KEITH CHEETHAM has been interes[...] as a regular on the stage in the [...] Sheffield. His lifelong love of Sha[...] Grammar school, where he became acqua[...] greatest plays and speeches. For ten years he ran his own theatre company to much acclaim.

Most of his life has been spent in the tourist industry. He organised a festival commemorating the 400th anniversary of the arrival of Mary Queen of Scots in Sheffield (in 1570), where she spent 14 years as a captive of Queen Elizabeth I. He has since written two books about the Scottish queen, and spent five years as Chairman of the English Branch of the Marie Stuart Society. In 1988, he was invited by the Heart of England Tourist Board to set up Black Country Tourism, and became its first Director. In this role he made regular trips to Warwickshire and learned more about the life of William Shakespeare.

Keith has previously written four books of history, including three published by Luath Press: *On the Trail of Mary Queen of Scots*, *On the Trail of The Pilgrim Fathers* and *On the Trail of John Wesley*.

Now available in Luath's *On the Trail of* series

On the Trail of
William Shakespeare

J. KEITH CHEETHAM

Luath Press Limited
EDINBURGH
www.luath.co.uk

First Published 2006
This edition 2007

ISBN (10): 1-905222-96-3
ISBN (13): 978-1-9-0522296-4

The paper used in this book is recyclable. It is made from
low chlorine pulps produced in a low energy, low emission manner
from renewable forests.

Line illustrations by David Middleton

Photographs by J. Keith Cheetham

Printed and bound by
Creative Print and Design, Ebbw Vale

Typeset in 10.5 point Sabon by
3btype.com

All the world's a stage,
And all the men and women merely players.
They have their exits and entrances:
And one man in his time plays many parts,
His acts being seven ages.

As You Like It, Act 2, Scene 7
William Shakespeare, 1564–1616

This book is dedicated to my grandchildren,
Oliver J. Dene and Emily R. Dene,
as a token of my love.

Acknowledgements

During the research, writing and compilation of this book, I have been given an enormous amount of help, guidance and assistance from many people. In addition, I have received much help from many Tourist Information Centres throughout Great Britain. However, I would, in particular, like to single out and thank most sincerely Dr Robert Bearman, Head of Archives and Local Studies at the Shakespeare Birthplace Trust Records Office in Stratford-upon-Avon, for his wise counselling, factual information, advice and checking of the manuscript, which have enabled me to complete the project.

I also owe a special debt of appreciation to the following people for their kind assistance:

Nicola Mills, The Shakespeare Birthplace Trust; staff at Shakespeare Houses in Stratford-upon-Avon and area; David Howells and staff, Royal Shakespeare Company; Will Sharpe, The Shakespeare Institute; T.P. Moore-Bridger, Headmaster, and Andy Palmer, King Edward VI Grammar School; Catherine Penn, Holy Trinity Parish Church – all in Stratford-upon-Avon; plus the staff and Marketing Department at Shakespeare's Globe Theatre, Bankside, London.

My special thanks are due to members of staff at the following tourist information centres – Jenny Camm and Penny Chambers, Stratford-upon-Avon TIC; and those at Chester, Coventry, Dunkeld, Fort William, Hereford, Ipswich, Oxford, Royal Leamington Spa, Shrewsbury, Stafford, Tewkesbury, Wakefield, Warwick, Windsor and York.

I should also like to thank the following persons or bodies for their assistance – David Miles, Historic Royal Palaces – Hampton Court Palace and the Tower of London; the National Trust staff at Baddesley Clinton, Coughton Court, Charlecote Park, Packwood House and Rufford Old Hall; English Heritage staff at Kenilworth Castle and Warkworth Castle; the Churches Conservation Trust and Dorothy Nicolle at St Mary Magdalene Church, Battlefield, Shrewsbury; Billesley Manor Hotel, near Stratford-upon-Avon, for access to Billesley Church; David McGrory, Coventry; David Hardwick, Bosworth Battlefield; Coventry Archives & Records Office; John Graver, Hoghton Tower, Lancashire; London Borough of Barnet – Archives & Local Studies Centre; Administrator, Scone Palace; Shrewsbury Civic Society; Shropshire Records & Archives Office; Stephanie Sherwood; staff at St Helen's Church, Bishopsgate, London; Staffordshire Records Office; Visitor Centre, York Minster; West Highland Museum, Fort William; Wolverhampton Central Library and Reference Library; and Worcestershire Records Office.

Finally, I should like to mention David Middleton, for his line drawings; Jim Lewis, cartographer; Tim West, editor; Tom Bee, designer; and my publishers at Luath Press, Audrey and Gavin MacDougall, for their continuing support and encouragement.

Contents

Abbreviations

CCT	Churches Conservation Trust
EH	English Heritage
HS	Historic Scotland
NT	The National Trust
RSC	Royal Shakespeare Company
SH	Shakespeare Houses
TIC	Tourist Information Centre

Addresses for the above organisations can be found on pages 176 to 178.

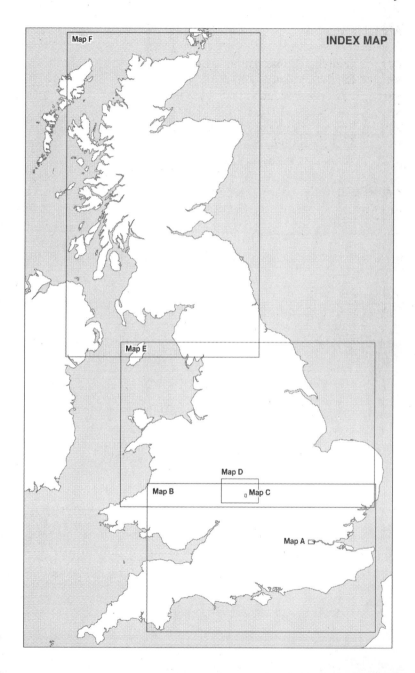

INDEX MAP

Map F

Map E

Map D

Map B

Map C

Map A

4

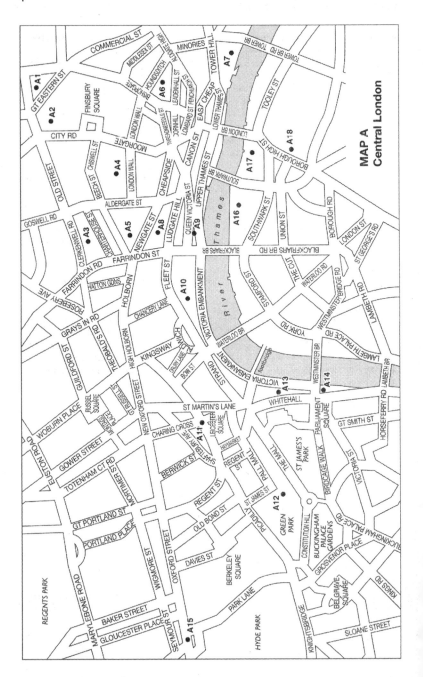

MAP A
Central London

Map A – Central London

A1– St Leonard's Church, Shoreditch
Burial place of actors Richard Burbage and
William Sly, and clown Richard Tarlton.

A2 – Site of The Theatre, Shoreditch
Playhouse owned by Burbage, where some
of Will's earlier plays were first presented.

A3 – St John's Gate, Clerkenwell
Part of medieval priory. Once the office of
the Master of the Revels, who licensed plays.

A4 – St Giles without Cripplegate Church
Burial place of Will's nephew, Edward,
illegitimate son of his brother, Edmund.

A5 – Smithfield
Execution place of Edward Arden, a relative
of Will's mother, Mary.

A6 – St Helen's Bishopsgate Church
It is thought Will worshipped here whilst living
in the parish. Splendid monuments.

A7 – Tower of London
Setting for *Henry VI, Part I* and *Richard III*.
Royal prison with historic associations.

**A8 – Site of Blackfriars theatre,
Playhouse Yard**
Site of former monastery. James Burbage
took over the property and used it as a
theatre.

A9 – Site of Baynard's Castle
Site of castle, by Puddle Dock, setting for
scenes in *Richard II* and *Richard III*.

A10 – Middle Temple Hall
Built 1572. Used for court performances.
The first performance of *Twelfth Night* was
held here.

**A11 – Shakespeare's Statue, Leicester
Square Gardens**
The statue of Will dominates as a centre-
piece in the gardens.

A12 – St James's Palace
Built 1531. Royal palace of Elizabeth I and
James I. Ben Jonson's plays presented here.

A13 – Banqueting House, Whitehall
Only surviving part of Whitehall Palace.
Once used for court masques and
performances.

**A14 – Westminster Abbey & Westminster
Hall**
Elaborate statue of Will in Poets Corner of
the abbey. Hall used as court in Tudor times.

A15 – Site of Tyburn, Marble Arch
Traditional place of execution, where Jesuit
priests Campion and Cottom met their
ends.

**A16 – Shakespeare's Globe Theatre,
Bankside**
Replica of first Globe Theatre. Close to the
original site, where Will staged many plays.

A17 – Southwark Cathedral
Well known to Will; burial place of his brother
Edmund and of other actors.

**A18 – George Inn, off Borough High
Street, Southwark**
Old coaching inn with balconies and yard.
Many teams of actors performed here.

6

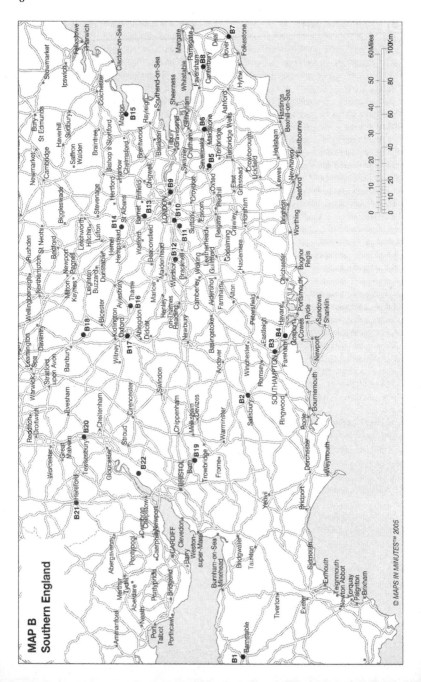

MAP B
Southern England

© MAPS IN MINUTES™ 2005

Map B – Southern England

B1 – Barnstaple, Devon
The King's Men made visits in 1605 & 1607 and performed by the River Taw.

B2 – Salisbury and Wilton House
The site of Buckingham's execution in *Richard III* was Salisbury market. *As You Like It* was performed by the King's Men for the Earl of Pembroke at Wilton, 1603.

B3 – Southampton, Hants
Henry V's departure point for France, for the Battle of Agincourt, 1415.

B4 – Titchfield Abbey EH, nr Fareham
Ruined home of Lord Southampton, with whom Shakespeare may have stayed.

B5 – Knole NT, nr Sevenoaks
Fine stately home. Contains furniture from the former Whitehall Palace.

B6 – Maidstone, Kent
The King's Men performed here in 1605-6.

B7 – Dover, Kent
Scenes in *King Lear* are set around the town. You can visit Shakespeare's Cliff.

B8 – Canterbury, Kent
Birthplace, in 1564, of poet and playwright Christopher Marlowe.

B9 – Greenwich, Greater London
Birthplace of Henry VIII in 1491. The Queen's Men performed here for Elizabeth I.

B10 – Richmond, Surrey
The Queen's Men played before Elizabeth I. She died here on 24 May 1603.

B11 – Hampton Court Palace, Surrey
Built 1516 by Cardinal Wolsey. Favourite palace of Elizabeth I and James I.

B12 – Windsor, Berkshire
The castle is an ancient royal stronghold. The town is the setting for *The Merry Wives of Windsor*.

B13 – Barnet, North London
Battle site depicted in *Henry VI, Part III*.

B14 – St Albans, Herts
Battle site in the Wars of the Roses, on 22 May 1455. Depicted in *Henry VI, Part II*.

B15 – Maldon, Essex
The King's Men sometimes performed here, possibly in the Moot Hall.

B16 – Thame, Oxfordshire
An actor in the Queen's Men was killed here just before they played in Stratford.

B17 – Oxford
Shakespeare is thought to have stayed at the Crown Tavern in Cornmarket Street.

B18 – Aynho, Northamptonshire
Jesuit John Somerville arrested here in 1583 after making allegations against Elizabeth I.

B19 – Bath, Somerset
The King's Men performed here, probably in the old Guildhall.

B20 – Tewkesbury, Gloucestershire
Site of a battle on 4 May 1471. Depicted in *Henry VI, Part III*.

B21 – Hereford
Execution site of Owen Tudor, after the Battle of Mortimer's Cross – *Henry VI, Part III*.

B22 – Berkeley Castle, Gloucestershire
Referred to by the Duke of York in *Richard II*.

8

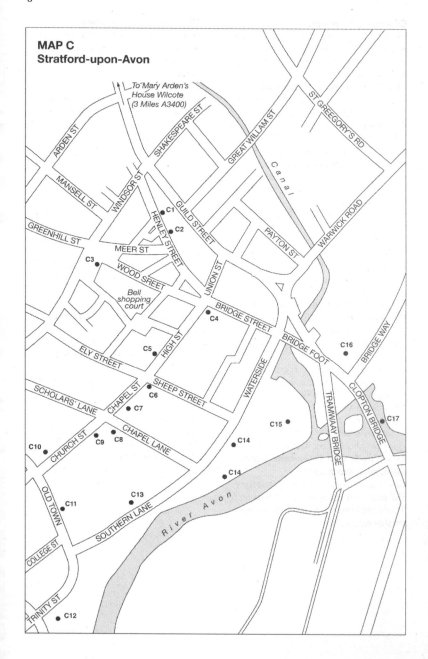

Map C – Stratford-upon-Avon

C1 – Shakespeare Centre
Home of the Shakespeare Birthplace Trust.
Built to celebrate the 400th anniversary of
Shakespeare's birth. Houses Birthplace Trust
Records Office & Archives.

C2 – Shakespeare's Birthplace SH
The half-timbered house where Shakespeare
was born in 1564. Includes an exhibition.

C3 – Market Place
Where John Shakespeare would have sold
wool, gloves and other products.

C4 – Judith Shakespeare's House
Where Will's daughter Judith lived with her
husband, Thomas Quiney. Now a retail outlet.

C5 – Harvard House SH
Once a butcher's shop owned by Thomas
Rogers, father-in-law to John Harvard.

C6 – Town Hall
Dedicated to Shakespeare by the actor David
Garrick in 1769. Look out for the statue of
Shakespeare at an upper elevation in Sheep
Street.

**C7 – Nash's House and foundations of
New Place SH**
Home of Shakespeare's granddaughter,
Elizabeth Hall and her husband, Thomas
Nash.

Adjacent is the site of the house in which
Shakespeare lived the last years of his life.
You can visit Knot Garden here.

C8 – Guild Chapel
Built by Hugh Clopton in late 15th century.
Important local building now used by the
grammar school. Public access permitted.

**C9 – King Edward VI Grammar School,
Guildhall & Almshouses**
Grammar school founded in 13th century.
Shakespeare probably went to school here.
Theatricals held in Guildhall. Half-timbered
almshouses adjoin.

C10 – Shakespeare Institute
Former home of Marie Corelli, authoress
and favourite of Queen Victoria. Now used
by University of Birmingham for
Shakespearean studies.

C11 – Hall's Croft SH
Home of Shakespeare's elder daughter,
Susanna, and her physician husband, Dr John
Hall.

C12 – Holy Trinity Church
Fine church dating from late 12th century.
Shakespeare was baptized and is buried
here.

C13 – The Other Place
Opened in 1974 for RSC as a third
performance area. Presents traditional and
modern works.

**C14 – Royal Shakespeare Theatre & Swan
Theatre**
Royal Shakespeare opened in 1932, designed
by Elizabeth Scott. Home of RSC. Swan
Theatre built in 1986 in the shell of the
former Shakespeare Memorial Theatre.

**C15 – The Shakespeare Monument,
Bancroft Gardens**
Presented by designer Lord Ronald
Sutherland Gower. Includes statues of
Shakespeare and four of his principal
characters (Hamlet, Lady Macbeth, Falstaff
and Prince Hal).

**C16 – Tourist Information Centre,
Bridgefoot**
Provides local, regional and national
information. Souvenir sales.

C17 – Clopton Bridge
Built in the reign of Henry VII by local
benefactor, Sir Hugh Clopton.

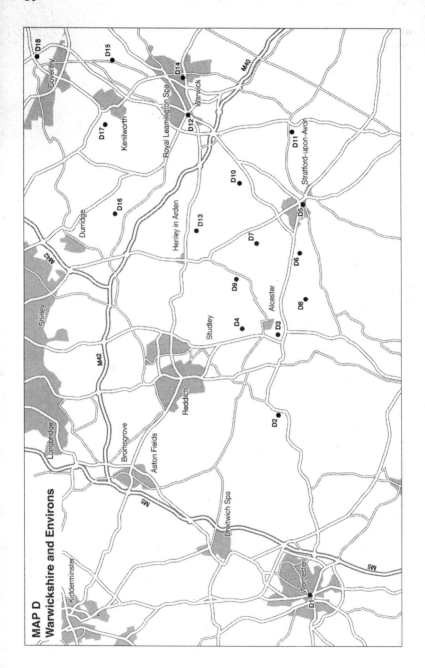

MAP D
Warwickshire and Environs

Map D – Warwickshire and Environs

D1 – Worcester
Will obtained his marriage licence here in 1582. See Worcester Cathedral.

D2 – Inkberrow, Worcs
Will is thought to have stayed at the Bull Inn en route to Worcester in 1582.

D3 – Alcester
Old market town close to Roman 'Ickneild Street'. Full of half-timbered houses.

D4 – Coughton Court NT
Family seat of Throckmortons since 1409. Links with Gunpowder Plot.

D5 – Stratford-upon Avon SH
Birthplace of William Shakespeare in 1564. With many Shakespeare Houses.

D6 – Shottery SH
Visit Anne Hathaway's Cottage, birthplace and family home of Shakespeare's wife.

D7 – Wilmcote SH
Visit Mary Arden's House and nearby Billesley Church, where Will may have wed.

D8 – Temple Grafton
Former St Andrew's Church is another place where Will may have wed.

D9 – Aston Cantlow
St John the Baptist church is thought to be where Shakespeare's parents were married.

D10 – Snitterfield
Ancestral home of Will's farming family. Visit St James's Church.

D11 – Charlecote Park NT
Elizabethan home of Lucy family. By tradition, Will poached game in the park.

D12 – Warwick
Has a splendid 14th century castle. You should also see St Mary's Church and Lord Leycester's Hospital.

D13 – Wootton Wawen and Henley-in-Arden
Henley is a small town, once in the Forest of Arden. Saxon Sanctuary at Wootton Wawen has a Forest of Arden exhibition and links with Somerville family.

D14 – Royal Leamington Spa
Elegant Regency spa town. See the Pump Room where the meeting was held in 1875 to discuss designs for the Royal Shakespeare Theatre in Stratford-upon-Avon.

D15 – Stoneleigh Abbey EH
Original 1154 Cistercian abbey. Corinthian style mansion with abbey gatehouse.

D16 – Baddesley Clinton NT
Former Catholic house which sheltered Jesuit priests and other recusants.

D17 – Kenilworth Castle EH
Impressive ruined castle, once home of Robert Dudley, Earl of Leicester. Famed for masques, pageants, jousting and visits by Elizabeth I.

D18 – Coventry, West Midlands
The setting for scenes in *Henry VI, Part III* and *Richard II*. The King's Men played twice here in 1603, probably at St Mary's Guildhall.

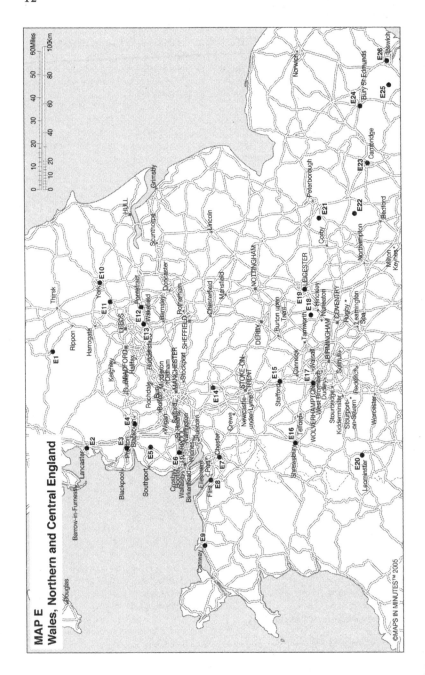

MAP E
Wales, Northern and Central England

©MAPS IN MINUTES™ 2005

Map E – Wales, Northern and Central England

E1 – Middleham Castle EH, Wensleydale, North Yorkshire
Favourite residence of Richard III. 12th century motte & bailey castle depicted in *Henry VI, Part III*.

E2 – Lancaster Castle, Lancashire
Sir Thomas Hesketh was imprisoned here for recusancy.

E3 – Tarnacre, nr Preston, Lancashire
Home of John Cottom, Jesuit and former schoolmaster at Stratford grammar school.

E4 – Hoghton Tower, nr Blackburn, Lancashire
Built by Sir Richard de Hoghton, supporter of recusants, who may have employed Shakespeare as a schoolmaster and actor.

E5 – Rufford Old Hall NT, nr Ormskirk, Lancashire
Home of Sir Thomas Hesketh, for whom Will may have worked. Hesketh kept a troupe of actors.

E6 – Knowsley, nr Liverpool, Lancashire
Home of Ferdinando, Lord Strange, who also employed a troupe of actors.

E7 – Chester
Bolingbroke was encamped at Chester prior to capturing Richard II at Flint Castle.

E8 – Flint Castle, Clwyd
Built by Edward I in 1277 and depicted in *Richard II* and *Henry IV, Part I*.

E9 – Conwy Castle, Conwy
In July 1399, Richard II arrived from Ireland to defend his throne at Flint.

E10 – York
Ancient city. Visit the Minster. Hotspur's head was displayed on Micklegate Bar in *Henry VI, Part III*.

E11 – Towton, nr Tadcaster, West Yorkshire
Battle site in the Wars of the Roses, in 1460. Depicted in *Henry VI, Part III*.

E12 – Pontefract Castle, Pontefract, West Yorkshire
In *Richard II, Act 5*, the overthrown King waits in his cell at 'Pomfret Castle'.

E13 – Sandal Castle, Wakefield, West Yorkshire
Site of the Battle of Wakefield. Depicted in *Henry VI, Part III*.

E14 – Gawsworth Hall, nr Macclesfield, Cheshire
Birthplace (in 1578) and childhood home of Lady Mary Fitton.

E15 – Stafford
The King's Men played in 1610 and 1613, probably in original Shire Hall.

E16 – Shrewsbury, Shropshire
Site of a battle depicted in *Henry IV, Part I*. The King's Men played in town. Visit nearby Condover, birthplace of Richard Tarlton, Elizabeth I's court jester.

E17 – Wolverhampton, West Midlands
Lady Mary Fitton was buried at St Michael & All Angels, Tettenhall. There is a statue of Admiral Richard Leveson in St Peter's Collegiate Church, city centre.

E18 – Bosworth Battlefield EH, Leicestershire
Battle site where Henry Tudor defeated Richard III. Scenes depicted in *Richard III*.

E19 – Leicester
Statue of Richard III in castle gardens.

E20 – Mortimer's Cross, nr Leominster, Herefordshire
Battle site of 2 February 1461. Depicted in *Henry IV, Part III*.

E21 – Site of Fotheringhay Castle, Northamptonshire
Birthplace of Richard III on 2 October 1452 and place of execution for Mary Queen of Scots on 8 February 1587. See nearby Church of St Mary the Virgin & All Saints.

E22 – Kimbolton Castle, nr St Neots, Huntingdonshire
Final residence of Catherine of Aragon. Depicted in *Henry VIII, Act 4*.

E23 – Cambridge
The King's Men regularly played Ben Jonson's *Volpone* in the Guildhall between 1603 and 1613.

E24 – Bury St Edmunds, Suffolk
Depicted in *Henry VI, Part II* and King John. See the remains of the abbey.

E25 – Hadleigh, Suffolk
The King's Men probably played in the 15th century Guildhall, which is still preserved.

E26 – Ipswich, Suffolk
The King's Men are thought to have played in the ancient Moot Hall on Cornhill.

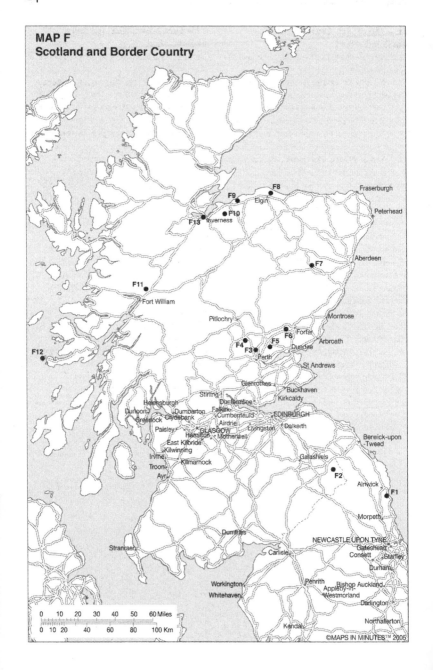

MAP F
Scotland and Border Country

©MAPS IN MINUTES™ 2005

F1 – Warkworth Castle EH, Northumberland

Northern stronghold of the Percy family. Features in *Henry IV, Parts I & II*.

F2 – Roxburgh Castle, nr Kelso, Border Region

Only earthworks remain of the castle demolished by the Scots. In *Edward III* King David of Scotland tries to woo the Countess of Salisbury at Roxburgh Castle.

F3 – Scone Palace, Perthshire

Home of the Earl of Mansfield. Early coronation site of Scottish Kings. A replica Stone of Scone marks the spot.

F4 – Birnam Wood, Perthshire

In Macbeth, the site at which Malcolm rallies his troops before attacking Macbeth at Dunsinane.

F5 – Hill of Dunsinane, Perthshire

Site of an Iron Age hill fort known as Macbeth's Castle, where, by tradition, Macbeth awaited Malcolm's troops. According to the play, Macbeth was killed here, but he actually died three years later at Lumphanan.

F6 – Glamis Castle, Angus

Malcolm II is said to have died here in 1034. Shakespeare names Macbeth as Thane of Glamis, but this is fictional.

F7 – Lumphanan, Aberdeenshire.

The site where the real Macbeth was defeated and killed by Malcolm Canmore, in August 1057.

F8 – Spynie Palace HS, nr Elgin, Moray

It is thought Duncan died here in 1040 in combat with Macbeth, who then became King of Scots.

F9 – Macbeth's Hillock, nr Forres, Moray

Fictional meeting place of Macbeth and Banquo with the three witches.

F10 – Cawdor Castle, Highland

Shakespeare names Macbeth as Thane of Cawdor, but the castle was actually built some centuries after Macbeth's death.

F11 – Banquo's Walk, nr Fort William, Highland

Traditional walkway alongside the River Lochy, near Muirshearlich in the Great Glen.

F12 – Isle of Iona HS, Argyll & Bute

Macbeth was taken to Iona Abbey, the traditional burial place of Scottish Kings, after his death in 1057.

F13 – Inverness

In the play, the site of Macbeth's Castle, where Duncan is murdered. The present castle is a 19th century replacement.

Introduction

WILLIAM SHAKESPEARE IS, without doubt, the greatest playwright and poet of all time and the best known in the English language. Yet for all his worldwide fame he still, to a large extent, remains an enigma whose background can never be entirely explored. Of course there is much that is known of the man but there are also many aspects of his life – especially the period known as the 'lost' years and his time in London – which have never been fully uncovered. Much of his 'life' has been mere speculation and assumption by a range of people including writers, professors of history and literature, those in the acting profession, and other experts in the Shakespearean field.

His name alone conjures up magical images of theatre and films associated with such renowned actor knights as Henry Irving, John Gielgud, Lawrence Olivier and Ian McKellen, coupled with the name of Kenneth Branagh. Distinguished leading ladies include Dames Flora Robson, Peggy Ashcroft, Judi Dench and eminent actresses such as Maggie Smith, Dorothy Tutin and Geraldine McEwan, all having made their mark in some of the great Shakespearean roles. Each, together with countless others, has made a major contribution to their art form by performances in some of the greatest roles ever written for the world stage.

To many, the name 'Shakespeare' brings back memories of school-days and the subjects of English literature and drama, and being given set passages or speeches from some of the Shakespearean plays to copy out or learn by heart for homework. Others, more fortunate, may well have taken part in school productions of some of the more popular plays written by the Bard. To most, it left some form of lasting impression, however vague, which would stay with them forever.

Let me make it clear that rather than being an appraisal of his works, this book's main object is to present to the reader an easy historical account of Shakespeare's life, coupled with information about the many locations associated therewith. In addition, I have included a selection of locations and sites depicted as backdrops in several of the more popular plays – especially those which can easily be seen by the general public. Most of these sites are already important visitor centres such as royal palaces, castles, stately homes or well-known battlefields.

Others are smaller, perhaps little-known sites, sometimes hidden away and off the beaten track.

Whatever your interest, I hope the book will provide a new insight into the life and times of the world's greatest scribe, maybe even encourage you to explore a little more into the hidden treasures of Britain's sometimes violent but always romantic history as you journey along – *On the Trail of William Shakespeare.*

J. Keith Cheetham
March 2006

PART ONE

THE LIFE OF WILLIAM SHAKESPEARE

CHAPTER I

Shakespeare's Ancestral Influences

WILLIAM SHAKESPEARE WAS born and grew up in the small market town of Stratford-upon-Avon (D5) in the countryside of Warwickshire, an area noted for its half-timbered thatched cottages, great stately homes and castles – for example those at Charlecote Park (D11), Baddesley Clinton (D16), Coughton Court (D4), Warwick and Kenilworth (D17). Middle England was already well established, with a rich heritage of English history and culture which provided Shakespeare a ready backdrop for many of his plays. The county of Warwickshire was more or less divided into two areas: the southern part consisted of open countryside dealing chiefly in agriculture; the northern section above the River Avon was mainly a wooded area, with clearings, cornfields and a number of small communities and dwellings situated in what was known as the Forest of Arden. This stretched across countryside approximately 17 miles (27km) long by 13 miles (21km) broad, and was made up of woodlands, large tracts of moor, unenclosed commons and heath land. South of the river lay a large open stretch of undulating farming country which was known as Feldon ('field-land'). It was heavily cultivated in medieval days and, to the south, merged with the Cotswolds.

The northern portion of the Forest is today rudely bisected from east to west by the busy M42 motorway. Only sparse clumps of trees remain of this once great area of woodland. By the 17th century, much of the woods had been felled for fuel to smelt iron in the new industrial towns which were springing up in the Midlands around the Birmingham area. This was prior to the advent of coal-mining. Wood was used extensively in the building of oak-timbered frameworks for houses, and spaces between the timbers were then filled-in with 'wattle and daub' or brick – both of which were manufactured in the region. Of the towns in the Forest of Arden, Henley-in-Arden (D13) and Alcester (D3) are the largest. The area was the setting for a number of pastoral scenes in Shakespeare's plays and poems.

So who was this man William Shakespeare and what was his family background? The surname seems to have originated in the Middle Ages, mainly from around Midland counties. Some of the family became involved with the guild of St Anne at Knowle, near Solihull, and went on to become leading inhabitants of Warwickshire. The name was found more frequently in this county than elsewhere during the 16th century, when twenty-four towns or villages were identified as having Shakespeare families. This rose to as many as thirty-four during the following century.

Snitterfield

Richard Shakespeare, grandfather of William, settled as a tenant farmer at a property in the quiet leafy village of Snitterfield (D10) sometime before 1525. He was known to have worshipped at the parish church of St James the Great until his death in 1560. The village was three miles (5km) north of Stratford, set in undulating countryside less than half way to Warwick. Richard's two sons, John and Henry, were born at Snitterfield and both later farmed there. The original Shakespeare property and land have only recently been discovered, sited at the corner of Bell Lane, which stretches down the hill from the church to where a ford crosses a stream. The actual property identified as having belonged to the Shakespeare family includes a section of a brick-built barn, possibly Tudor, with small windows and timbering. It was here that Richard Shakespeare and, later, his two sons, were tenants on some one hundred acres of agricultural land owned by Robert Arden of nearby Wilmcote (D7). John Shakespeare, father of William, moved to Stratford-upon-Avon around 1550 whilst Henry continued to live at the Snitterfield property until his death in 1591. (He was excommunicated by the Church ten years earlier for refusing to pay his tithes.)

Although parish records at Snitterfield only began in 1561 – the year after the death of Richard Shakespeare – the village dates back to Saxon times, maybe earlier, and derives its name from 'Snytenfeld' meaning 'place of a snipe'. The registers contain several references to members of Richard's family and it is assumed he is buried somewhere in the churchyard along with his wife. Richard's grandson, William Shakespeare, may well have walked from Stratford to visit his uncle Henry and aunt Margaret, so would have been familiar with the local parish church and other local buildings. Both manor and church records also refer to one Thomas Shakesper – possibly another son of Richard – and the register for 1595 records the death of his wife Johanna.

Origins of the church date back to the 13th century, when the chancel, south nave arcade and aisle were built, from local lias ragstone. Though it is strongly buttressed, the walls lean slightly outwards. The font, tower and north nave arcade and aisle date from the 14th century but the building underwent much restoration during Victorian times. The spacious chancel is less than ten feet shorter than the nave, its most prominent feature being the large east window, which includes heavy tracery. Notable are the Jacobean oak communion rails of 1630, carved with running foliage, and two short ranges of carved stalls near to the altar, constructed around 100 years earlier. The font dates from the 14th century, which gives rise to speculation that it could well have been used at the baptisms of various members of the Shakespeare family. Snitterfield has a charm of its own, with winding lanes and a number of half-timbered houses dotted around a rather sprawling community.

Stratford-upon-Avon
Tel: 0870 160 7930 – Stratford TIC

When John Shakespeare moved to Stratford-upon-Avon he most likely served an apprenticeship to become a glove maker by trade prior to being accepted by the Company of Skinners and Tailors. He both lived and worked in a shop in Henley Street, was ambitious, and anxious to establish himself as a local tradesman. It was thought that John was a tenant in the property from 1552, possibly earlier. However, documentary evidence has since revealed that John acquired this site in two separate dealings, the major part of the house being purchased in 1556, the remainder in 1575.

The main industry in the town was malting, though about a third of the population processed malt themselves as a side-line. As in neighbouring towns, each occupation had earlier formed its own company, and skinners and tailors were no exception. In 1597 most men in Stratford were members of one or other of the trade companies. For years the close proximity of the Cotswold hills had been a ready supplier of wool for the cloth industry, but trade started to diminish around the 1590s causing unemployment amongst local townsfolk. However, there was expansion in the gloving industry centred on Stratford, with the result that John Shakespeare's business began to thrive. As well as trading in gloves he dealt in grain, wool and other commodities. He was also involved in money-lending.

Stratford has always enjoyed a beautiful setting – especially colourful in the autumn – where ducks and swans glide peacefully alongside pleasure craft on the River Avon to the delight of many visitors. It is a market town which the whole world regards as quintessentially English. That so many wonderful timber houses have survived for over four centuries is due in part to a timely decline in Stratford's fortunes whilst other places were demolishing and rebuilding themselves. It had to be content with its existing buildings, many of which are still as Shakespeare would have known them. They have survived the passage of time along with the vibration of heavy traffic and the tramping of millions of pairs of feet down the attractive streets and thoroughfares. There are lanes of antique and speciality shops, plus quaint teashops and ancient inns complete with dark beams and white-washed walls – often decked with horse brasses – with inlaid or carved paneling and log fires.

The town is situated more or less midway along the course of the Avon as it winds its way through Warwickshire. The river rises at Naseby in Northamptonshire and joins the River Severn at Tewkesbury. There was a settlement at Stratford in the Bronze Age when the site became a river-crossing. This is described in Stratford's name, *'straet'* being a Roman road, and 'ford' referring to its crossing of the Avon (Celtic for 'river'). There is evidence of both Roman and Saxon occupation. The settlement grew up beside the ford and local inhabitants smelted iron and lead, obtaining wood for charcoal from the nearby Forest of Arden. They also made pottery. In AD 693 there was a minster, which probably stood on the site of, or close by to, the present Holy Trinity parish church (C12). The nearby area is still called Old Town, which more or less indicates the site of the original community to the south of the town centre. When the Domesday Book was written in 1086, Stratford was mentioned as a manor owned by the Bishop of Worcester, in whose diocese the town remained until the early 20th century. It now falls under the diocese of Coventry (D18).

With its fine geographical position, Stratford has long been an important crossroads for routes across the country. This has been the case since 1196, when the town was first granted a charter for its weekly market by Richard 1 and enjoyed a growing popularity as a location for fairs and markets. The original cattle market was probably held in Rother Street but, over the years, moved to other locations. It is now more or less back where it started in Rother Street and takes place every Friday. Three market crosses once graced the town – one for local butchers in Chapel Street, another for suppliers of dairy foods in front of the Guild Chapel, and the third – the High Cross – for the sale of gloves at the junction of High Street and Bridge Street (c3) (it was from here that John Shakespeare would probably have sold his products. The base of this medieval cross can be seen in the exhibition at Shakespeare's Birthplace (c2)).

The town's historic fairs are commemorated every year on 12 October with the traditional Mop Fair – the last surviving – originally an event where local folk sought employment from prospective employers. With the building of the Clopton Bridge (c17) between 1480 and 1490 by Hugh Clopton, one of the town's greatest benefactors, better access was established between northern and southern routes. It was the only river crossing for many miles. The bridge today has fourteen arches but originally there were five more in the direction of the town. Hugh became Lord Mayor of London in 1492, having originally gone there as a boy and made his fortune as a mercer, or dealer in textiles. He returned to Stratford a rich man and decided to invest some of his money in his native town for the benefit of the local population. He enlarged the Guild Chapel (c8) and built both the Clopton Bridge and one of the finest houses in the town, which was for his own personal use. The bridge still carries heavy traffic out of the town on the A422 to Banbury and other southern routes. The house was constructed of brick and timber and named New Place (c7) but is now demolished. The garden remains and both it and the adjacent Nash's House (c7) are administered by the Birthplace Trust and are open to the public. (A smaller and narrower brick-built bridge of nine arches was later erected across the river in 1823, its purpose being to carry the horse-drawn tramway which originally transported raw materials from Stratford wharf to Morton-in-the Marsh. The bridge is now a pedestrian walkway to the south bank of the River Avon and nearby Stratford Butterfly Farm.)

A flourishing guild or fraternity of the Holy Cross was established during the Middle Ages and a license was granted to build a chapel in 1269 by Bishop Godfrey Giffard of Worcester. The guild, founded by Robert de Stratford, included many leading townsfolk of both sexes, and people from other parts of the county. As well as looking to the town's welfare by making charitable donations, supporting the local grammar school and almshouses, its main purpose was to employ priests to pray for the souls of its various members. The Guild of the Holy Cross was amalgamated with the guilds of Our Lady and St John Baptist in 1403, and was the ruling body of Stratford until the time of the

Dissolution of the Chantries by Edward VI in 1547, when its possessions became Crown property. Only the school was spared. A petition was sent to the boy King to incorporate the town as a borough, and to hand back the Guild properties to the local authority, in order to continue the facilities of the school and almshouses plus the maintenance of the Clopton Bridge. The petition was finally accepted in 1553, from which time Stratford was run by a body of its own, the Corporation, which included a bailiff, burgesses and aldermen.

In the early 1550s, conditions of hygiene were most undesirable. Water supplies into the town, fed by local streams and wells, often became contaminated. Little provision was available for waste disposal, and livestock markets were held in the open streets, where cattle were slaughtered. The removal of animal and human waste caused severe problems. In consequence, the local council provided refuse heaps on the edge of the town where human wastage, offal and other garbage could be dumped. John Shakespeare angered local officials by making his own refuse dump (or dung hill) in Henley Street, for which he was fined the princely sum of one shilling by the magistrate. He should have used the common 'muck heap' on the road leading out of the town. The danger of creating his own dump was that it attracted rats, which helped to spread the dreaded bubonic plague. His action temporarily left a black mark against his name – not a bright outlook for such an ambitious man as John Shakespeare.

Wilmcote

In the meanwhile, John had fallen in love with Mary Arden, the youngest of eight daughters from the first marriage of John's own Snitterfield landowner, Robert Arden of Wilmcote. She was born sometime in the 1530s. Wilmcote is situated 3 miles (5km) north west of Stratford and a similar distance from John's home village of Snitterfield. The Arden family dated back to pre-1066, took their name from the Forest of Arden, and already had their own coat of arms. Robert was a some-what prosperous landlord, owning properties and land in Wilmcote, Snitterfield and elsewhere. In 1550, when he was deciding on how his estate should be divided in the future, four of his daughters were still unmarried. However, on the death of his first wife, Robert re-married a widow, Agnes Hill, who already had four children of her own. He died in 1556 and was buried at Aston Cantlow (D9), leaving to his youngest daughter, Mary, a bequest of six pounds, a six-acre farm called Asbies, and a share in the Snitterfield site. This ensured she was provided with a handsome dowry to woo any prospective husband. The man she chose was John Shakespeare and the couple were married around 1557, possibly in the Church of St John the Baptist in the village of Aston Cantlow, 7 miles (11km) from Stratford. After the wedding, Mary and John set up home together at his existing house in Henley Street, Stratford.

Aston Cantlow

A priest is mentioned as being at Aston Cantlow in the Domesday Book, which indicates there was a church by 1086. It is thought that the existing building – the Church of St John the Baptist – goes back to the 13th century and it may have been built on the site of an earlier Saxon place of worship. A castle was built close to the River Alne after the Norman Conquest but was destroyed in 1265 when the barons, under Simon de Montfort, were defeated at the Battle of Evesham. It is possible that much of the stone from the former castle was incorporated into the building of the new church. During the reign of King John (1199–1216), the land was owned by William de Cantilupe but much of the chancel, nave and parts of the lower tower date from the reign of Henry III (1216–72). One member of the Cantilupe family – Thomas de Cantilupe (1218–82) – was a priest in the church at Aston Cantlow, went on to become Bishop of Hereford and, later, served as Lord Chancellor to Henry III. He was the last Englishman to be canonized before the Reformation. The village is therefore one of only two parishes in England to have had a saint as a priest. His family gave the settlement the second part of its name.

St John the Baptist church is built on a pleasant site, shaded by giant yew trees and surrounded by a range of half-timbered buildings. An ancient carving of the Nativity can be seen above the north door. The upper part of the tower is Perpendicular but the great porch is by the Victorian architect William Butterfield, who also restored the nave and other parts in 1850. Evidence of stained glass windows by Charles Kempe, the Victorian artist, can be seen in the chancel and guild chapel. In the south wall of the chancel – which noticeably leans outwards – are seats for three priests and an ancient bishop's chair incorporating a 'green man' – a pagan fertility symbol often found in Christian churches.

Undoubtedly, to most visitors the Shakespearean link is the most interesting aspect of the church. In the north west corner is an octagonal font dating from the 15th century, which could possibly have been used for the baptism of Mary Arden. Her birthplace, thought to have been at Wilmcote, formed part of the ecclesiastical parish of Aston Cantlow but, unfortunately, parish records do not exist to prove the baptismal ceremony actually took place there. It is highly probable she married John Shakespeare in the church in 1557. Again, church registers did not begin until three years later in 1560, so there is no positive proof of this either. Nevertheless, no other building in the area can lay full claim to this particular event. It has been suggested that the wedding celebrations continued at the nearby picturesque King's Head Inn but the building is of a later period. A more likely venue is the Guild House, which dates back to the early 16th century. One can only speculate on these matters.

Mary Arden's House and Palmer's Farm, Wilmcote (SH)

Tel: 01789 293455

Mary Arden's House

Mary Arden was brought up in quite a well-to-do family. Her father, Robert, ran a mixed farm with eight oxen, two bullocks, seven cows, four weaning calves, pigs and poultry. If Mary or any of her sisters wished to ride or be driven into Stratford there were four horses and three colts in the stables. The family home was, according to Robert's own inventory, well furnished and decorated as befitted a gentleman yeoman farmer of his standing. Mary would have played a full part in her father's farm and, along with her sisters, would have helped with cooking, washing, brewing, looking after the animals, and many other agricultural and domestic chores. For many years the property was called Glebe Farm. The complex remained a working farm until the 1930s and in 1968 was purchased by the Shakespeare Birthplace Trust, who maintained its essentially rural character.

For years, historians, writers and everyone else went under the misapprehension that Mary Arden lived in the house now known as

Palmer's Farm. By tradition it was always assumed that the black and white half-timbered building was where William Shakespeare's mother spent her girlhood up to the time of her marriage to John Shakespeare. However, in 2000, from research carried out by the Shakespeare Birthplace Trust, new and unknown documentary evidence revealed it was actually the house next door – Glebe Farm – where the Arden family had lived! Glebe Farm was re-named Mary Arden's House and the building formerly known by that name was re-titled Palmer's Farm. It is so called after a neighbour of the Ardens, Adam Palmer, who re-built the property in the late 16th century. He was a close friend of Robert and an overseer of his will. It was a happy coincidence that the Birthplace Trust owned Glebe Farm (it had been bought by the Church during the 18th century) and had already incorporated it as part of the popular tourist site.

The complex is made up of the house and farm plus a number of old outbuildings and barns in which rural collections owned by the Shakespeare Countryside Museum are displayed.

In summer the garden of Palmer's Farm is bursting with flowers and herbs, whilst the approach to Mary Arden's House is through a typical country garden where redcurrant bushes heavy with fruit mingle with poppies and foxgloves. The area around Wilmcote is still very much as it would have been in William Shakespeare's day, when he paid regular visits to see his Arden grandparents, Robert and Agnes. Undoubtedly the village and its surroundings had a major influence on his life and they were introduced in some of his later writings. Will would have observed the rural nature of the country-side – the trees, plants and crops, as well as local bird life. Alongside falcons and hawks he would have spotted the smaller birds which nested in the hedgerows, walls, woods and river banks of his home county. These included larks and mallards, lapwing, wren and robin. He was to weave descriptions of them all into his future work as a writer.

Entering the complex we pass into the Rick yard of Palmer's Farm, which contains twelve 'staddle stones'. A wooden frame would once have been placed over these for the building of ricks of straw and hay, in order to lift them free from the scourge of vermin, away from damp ground, or possibly to protect them from a dank atmosphere. Around the yard are various items once used in agriculture and other aspects of rural and domestic life. These are neatly displayed under protective cover from inclement weather, and include two Romany gypsy caravans and some farm wagons. A second yard contains a small barn with a horse-powered cider mill and an attractive dovecote with over 650 nesting holes. There is also an open-fronted byre. Water was obtained from wells, one being situated where the present water pump stands.

From the farmyard we enter Palmer's Farm via a rear door. The south face of the house has a 'chocolate box' timber-framed black and white facade and most probably was the building's frontage. The oldest part of this house is the wing, which has been dated back to around 1569 and has decorative herringbone timbers. As you approach the hall and kitchen, notice a cross-passage which was built around 1580 and was a replacement for an earlier construction. There is a large open fireplace in the kitchen together with a display of pewter tableware and Elizabethan cooking utensils. Meals were served in the hall, where the family would come together of an evening to eat, relax and discuss the events and chores of the day. In warmer weather these conversations would probably have taken place around a large family dining table placed neatly in the centre of the room. In winter, the family would have nestled close to the fireplace for warmth. Tiny windows in the room let in very little daylight and, even at nightfall, there were only rush light candles to offer any form of lighting. Adjacent to the hall is the dairy, where visitors can take a look at butter and cheese-making implements, as used in Shakespeare's time. The floor is sunken and the room is situated at the back of the house facing north, and is therefore much cooler than other parts.

After a meal was over, the family would retire to the parlour, which is approached by some steps to the ground floor. The room is simply appointed with oak furniture, including a 16th century chest with carved panels and a large 17th century bread ark. There are four upstairs bedroom and storage areas containing typical bedroom furnishings of the period, plus a rare truckle bed with castors which, when not in use, could easily have been hidden away under the main bed. There was little privacy as there was no corridor and one room led into another. Some of the old beams are rather low and taller persons should take care when viewing this part of the house.

At the rear of Palmer's Farm – across the other side of the farmyard – is a stable where farm animals were kept. Adjacent is the great barn, which includes more items from the Countryside Museum collection, so arranged as to illustrate the various types of farm equipment or machinery used in each of the seasons. Elizabethan pastimes popular with country folk are also depicted, both of a creative and sporting nature, including displays of falconry. There is evidence that William

Shakespeare was active in falconry and, in order to tame the birds, always allowed them plenty of food and sleep. Some of his plays and sonnets make reference to the sport of falconry.

We enter the former Glebe Farm (now Mary Arden's House) from across a small field. From the outside, it is not quite as attractive as Palmer's Farm, mainly because some of its exterior walls were rebuilt in brick, possibly in the 18th century. Mary Arden was born here when the house was about twenty years old; it was also here that Shakespeare's grandfather, Robert Arden, died, and both his will and inventory have survived the passage of time to provide evidence of his mode of living in such a property. Entrance is by a door into the living room: part of the main section of the house, built in 1514. In here is an original fireplace and hearth close to an old oven. Seated on a chair is a three-dimensional model of an old lady plucking a hen, surrounded by traditional furniture and farmhouse utensils. Just off the main living room is a dairy, built in the early 16th century. As one would expect, it houses equipment – churns, cream bowls and a milking stool used in the making of dairy products such as cheese and butter – and again is situated on the north side of the house.

Beyond the living room is a parlour – reserved for more formal occasions – and a cold store for the preservation of game, foodstuffs and other perishable commodities. The family would have kept their best furniture and items of value or ancestral significance in the parlour. On the first floor is a series of rooms – formerly bedchambers or storage areas – and it is here that the farm's original timber-framed structure can best be identified. Tree-ring analysis has shown that most of the timbers were felled circa 1514. Descending to ground level, notice the back kitchen and scullery where a typical wash-day of 100 years ago is depicted. Finally, leaving the house we reach the stable, great barn and other outbuildings, in which the visitor can see displays about local rural trades – such as the blacksmith, wheelwright and carpenter – and the uses of timber and stone gathered from the Forest of Arden. Regular demonstrations are given of the skills of birds of prey and the complex is completed by a circular walk and nature trail on which one can see examples of local flora and fauna.

Few love to hear the scenes they love to act

Pericles, Act 1, Scene 1

Some four years after the 'muck heap' fiasco in Stratford, the episode faded into the background and John Shakespeare began to move into public life and office. He was one of two people described as 'able and discreet' who were chosen to be tasters of ale to check that local beer was both wholesome and pitched at the right price. They also had to check on the substance and weight of local bread. Failure to comply could lead to being fined, whipped, put in the town stocks or even plunged into the River Avon on a 'ducking' stool – a punishment also meted out to villains and nagging wives!

By 1558, the year after he was married, John Shakespeare had been elected one of four constables whose responsibilities included the control of street rioting and subsequent arrest of offenders. A few weeks prior to this appointment the young couple – John and Mary – had their first child, Joan. Sadly she died shortly afterwards, and her name was later given to their fifth child. Another daughter, Margaret, was born in 1562, but died in the following year. Six more children were born and all except one, Anne, were to live on into adulthood. Each was born at the house in Henley Street in the period 1558–80.

Their third child was a boy, William, and it is generally accepted that he was born on 23 April 1564 (St George's Day – St George being the patron saint of England). This would mean William died on his own birthday – rather like the character of Cassius in his play *Julius Caesar* – the date being Tuesday 23 April 1616. The new child was destined not only to bring fame and fortune to his home town of Stratford but also to become one of the greatest Britons of all time. It was the beginning of a phenomenon in both English literature and language.

O, how bitter a thing it is to look into happiness through another man's eyes!

As You Like It, Act 5, Scene 2

CHAPTER 2

A Stratford Boyhood

WITHIN THE FIRST few days of his birth, William Shakespeare was baptised at the font in Holy Trinity Church which stands peacefully beside the River Avon in Stratford, its graceful spire rising above the crops of woodland and foliage. The baptismal entry was written in Latin and reads *April 26: Gulielmus filius Johannes Shakspere*. This church was also to become Shakespeare's last resting place 52 years later.

A few months after his birth there was an outbreak of the bubonic plague in Stratford and those infected systematically had the doors of their houses painted red in order to protect others from disease. As a precaution, his mother may have taken the infant William away from the town – either to her own former home at Wilmcote or, possibly, to the nearby village of Clifford Chambers (the half-timbered pre-Reformation manor house close to St Helen's Parish Church has been suggested as a place where they may have escaped the pestilence). Wilmcote is the far likelier option as Mary's close relatives could have assisted her in the chores of motherhood.

The Catholic Mary Tudor had died six years earlier and been succeeded

It is a wise father that knows his own child

The Merchant of Venice, Act 2, Scene 2

as queen by her half-sister, the Protestant Elizabeth I. This gave rise to another religious revolution and, by the mid-16th century, England was again at war with herself. The Crown of England was on a collision course with the Pope in Rome, originally charted by one of the most repellant monarchs ever to rule the country, Henry VIII, when he broke with Catholicism and founded the Church of England in 1534, which started the Dissolution. Prior to this, the Established Church in England had always been Roman Catholic. King Henry automatically seized existing monasteries and desecrated, destroyed or sold them off to raise money, whilst he converted cathedrals and churches into Church of

England properties. He left no stone unturned in ridding the country of any reminders of Popery but, ironically, requested on his deathbed that he be given the last rites.

After Henry's death England continued as a Protestant nation under the rule of his son and heir, the boy King Edward VI, but the country reverted to Catholicism when Edward's elder sister, Mary Tudor – the next in line for the throne – succeeded him. Much persecution of supporters on either side of the religious platform took place during these reigns and many were burned at the stake as religious heretics. Although there was a change back to the Anglican Church when Elizabeth I ascended as Sovereign in 1558, many former Catholics still had strong leanings toward their old religion, and continued to practice the Sacrament in private. John Shakespeare is thought to have been one such Catholic.

Although its College dissolved, one church which did manage to survive the Dissolution was the former Collegiate Church of the Holy and Undivided Trinity in Stratford. Let us pause for a few moments to learn something of this wonderful place of worship and the pleasing epitome of English ecclesiastic architectural styles which makes it, undisputedly, one of England's finest parish churches.

Holy Trinity Church, Stratford
Tel: 01789 266316

Holy Trinity Church

Ideally, the first-time visitor to Stratford should start with a glance downriver from the nine-arch pedestrian tramway bridge towards the Royal Shakespeare Theatre. Beyond, you see a distant view of Holy Trinity Church, its elegant tower and spire a landmark for miles around. This is a good starting place for a walk through the water meadows, down to the church. Those who wish to look around its interior will need to follow the road named Waterside, which leads into Southern Lane, passing the entrance to the Swan Theatre (C14), and on to Mill Lane. Alternatively, to see the stately medieval church from across the river, you should continue across the bridge and take the pleasant riverside walk through the recreation grounds to a point where you can get an uninterrupted view across the Avon, often busy with colourful pleasure craft and fishermen. From here you get a clear perspective of the cruciform building, elegant tower and slender spire.

To enter the churchyard from Mill Lane, you walk along The Churchway, a paved footpath under an avenue of lime trees which leads to the north porch. It is an unusual walk, passing many ancient gravestones; especially picturesque in late autumn with the various tints of shedding leaves. The trees to the left of the path represent the twelve tribes of Israel and those on the right depict the twelve Apostles of Jesus Christ. Eleven of these are limes but Judas Iscariot is represented by a holly bush. A further lime tree is set back to depict Matthias. On reaching the door of the north porch, the visitor's eye is often drawn towards an unusual Sanctuary door knocker. The effigy of an ancient character grasps the knocker in its mouth and this undoubtedly would have been familiar to Shakespeare. It was used by fugitives fleeing from the law, who would find sanctuary in the church for up to 37 days prior to any trial. This would have given them some time and space to contact any possible defence witnesses to assist with their cause or case. The alternative would have been to be thrown into gaol to await sentence. Here in the church, fugitives were able to receive food, lodging and alms from the monks, priests or other members of the clergy in residence. Near the sanctuary door is a cedar tree, almost opposite the west door, which was taken as a sapling from the Garden of Gethsemane by the Reverend Chafy Chafy in 1872.

It is from the north porch that many visitors eagerly make their way into the nave and towards the chancel to see the William Shakespeare memorial and grave. Several other members of his family are also buried here. Tourists usually take a quick glance around this one area in the sanctuary, maybe make a short stop in the souvenir shop, then hurriedly depart to seek out another Shakespearean landmark, without taking a few minutes to look at the other parts of this exquisite building. It is such a great pity, for Holy Trinity Church is a most historic place, dating back to the 13th century, with some wonderful architectural features, ancient tombs and memorials, and some of the finest stained glass windows in the whole of Warwickshire.

The first indication of the site as a place of worship in Stratford is in a charter of AD 845 signed by Beorthwulf, King of Mercia, who granted privileges to the small minster church in the town, which was possibly of wooden construction and lay close to the present building. The transepts were built around 1210 – maybe as part of an earlier structure – and the pillars in the nave were erected about 1280. Arches were built a century later, conforming to a great cruciform plan when the existing church was recorded in 1332. This was the date that John de Stratford, Archbishop of Canterbury and Lord Chancellor of England, founded a chantry for five priests in the south aisle chapel, dedicated to Thomas à Becket. It led to its confirmation as a college for priests by King Henry V in 1415, the same year as the Battle of Agincourt. At that time the church was first styled a 'collegiate church' and the rector was renamed 'Warden of the College'. (Until the Reformation the church had equal status with St Mary's Church in Warwick.) The clerestory was included in the late 15th century, completing one of the best examples of Perpendicular architecture to be seen anywhere.

The original foundation of the church was later extended by the Guild of the Holy Cross, founded in 1269. Much of the roof timbering dates back to medieval times but the tie beams which separate the twelve bays are modern. The chancel, with its carved misericords, clerestory, north porch, west window and tower, was completed between 1480 and 1520.

Like many other churches, Holy Trinity suffered greatly under the Reformation – the rood and chantry chapels were done away with, intricate carvings were smashed, and much stained glass was vandalised. In the next century a wooden spire was built above the tower, but was replaced by the present stone one in 1763. Many other embellishments and additions to church furniture were made during the Victorian period, some of which have been retained, the organ being moved to its present site in 1889. In the south transept is the 'American Window', a gift in 1896 from the US Ambassador, which depicts both American and English notables venerating the Virgin and Child. One of the latest additions to the building is a new altar made of American white oak, which was installed in 1998.

At the east end of the north aisle is the ancient Clopton Chapel, formerly the Lady Chapel, the burial place of the Clopton family, which is dedicated to the patron saints of local guilds, St Mary and St John. It includes the canopied altar tomb prepared for Sir Hugh Clopton, who was actually buried in London in 1496. There are also the impressive altar tomb and alabaster effigies of William Clopton (d.1592) and his wife Agnes and, above them, a carved and painted frieze showing their seven children. The excellent carvings on the tomb of George Carew, Earl of Totnes and Baron Clopton (1555–1629), and his wife, Joyce, in the same chapel, led it to be described as 'the finest Renaissance tomb in Europe.' Carew was a former commander in the English navy who became Master in Ordnance to James I.

The font in the nave is actually a copy of what is thought to be the original, now in the chancel, at which Shakespeare was baptised. This particular font was at some time displaced from the church and was re-discovered in a local garden during the 19th century. In 1823, it was restored to its rightful setting in Holy Trinity Church. The chancel also has a wonderful east window in stained glass, depicting the 'Adoration of the Crucified Christ' by angels and saints. Just beneath the window and high altar is the highlight of any visit for tourists – the last resting place of William Shakespeare. The parish register records the burial on 25 April 1616 and reads *Will Shakspere, gent*. He was buried within the sanctuary of the chancel.

Alongside Shakespeare's tombstone, within the Sanctuary rail, lie the graves of his wife, Anne; his eldest daughter, Susanna; her husband, Dr John Hall; and Thomas Nash, who married Shakespeare's grand-daughter, Elizabeth Hall. Gazing down on these individual memorials is the bust of William Shakespeare, from his own memorial on the north wall of the chancel. The sculptor was Gerard Johnson (or Janssen), an Anglo-Flemish mason of London, and the work was completed a few years after Shakespeare's death, during his wife's lifetime. She may have approved of the likeness. It is surmounted by his coat of arms. The first two lines of his epitaph can be translated as *In judgment a Nestor, in wit a Socrates, in art a Virgil. The earth covers him, the people mourn him, Olympus has him*. Shakespeare's face on the bust appears rather bloated and is likely to depict his appearance in later years, unlike the one authentic portrait of the famous playwright and poet in his heyday in London, engraved by Martin Droeshout and prefixed to the *First Folio* of 1623, the first collected edition of Shakespeare's plays, sonnets and poems. (Will's great friend and colleague, fellow actor-dramatist Ben Jonson, who wrote the 'Lines to the Reader' in accompaniment to this engraving in the *Folio*, was in complete agreement with the two editors, John Heminges and Henry Condell. It is most unlikely that these three close colleagues would have sanctioned the inclusion of a false representation of the Bard.) Restoration of the memorial took place in 1974 following research of the original colouration. It shows Will with a quill pen poised in his right hand, ready to write. The left lies upon a sheet of paper. The feathered quill is replaced every year at the ceremony held to mark his birthday on 23 April, when wreaths of colourful flowers are laid on all the Shakespeare family graves in the sanctuary.

Shakespeare's Birthplace, Stratford (SH)
Tel: 01789 201823

The house in Henley Street, Stratford, in which
William Shakespeare was born is a
half-timbered building of a type
common in the town during
Elizabethan times. As with similar houses, it was built with
local materials: green oak for
the framework, extracted
from the nearby Forest of
Arden, and blue lias stone footings quarried
at Wilmcote. No record of its building actually exists
but, judging from architectural features, one can assume that most of
the property dates from the early 16th century.

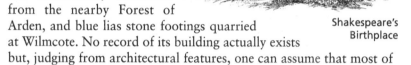

Shakespeare's
Birthplace

When John Shakespeare took over the house it was divided into
two separate parts: a place of residence for the Shakespeare family,
and an adjoining workshop or store for glove making and other work.
Rooms today are furnished in the style of Elizabethan and Jacobean
periods and contain items common to middle-class homes in Stratford
during Shakespeare's time. Records survive which prove the workshop
section of the house stayed in family ownership until 1806. Soon after
John Shakespeare died in 1601, William leased the workshop to an
innkeeper and it became known as the Maidenhead Inn. The inn was
used for recruiting and billeting by Parliamentarians during the Civil
War and, later, became known as the Swan and Maidenhead. The
adjoining residential part of the property stayed in the family until
1896 – it was passed down by Joan Hart, younger sister of William, who
lived there until her death in 1646. The Birthplace is first mentioned
as such on the earliest street map of Stratford, compiled and published
in 1759 by Samuel Winter. By the early 19th century, the former
Shakespeare family home had become a butcher's shop. It was not until
the mid-19th century that visitors began to arrive in large numbers
through the advent of the railway.

All tours of the Birthplace begin at the Visitor Centre, which
includes an introductory exhibition about Shakespeare's life and
career in both Stratford and London, and some family background. It
also contains a number of interesting artifacts such as the record of

Will's baptism in the parish register of 1564, a 15th/16th century desk from Stratford's King Edward VI Grammar School, details of Will's marriage, a scale model of the Globe Theatre, a first edition copy of his collected plays, and details of his will. From the Visitor Centre we cross the garden to the Birthplace itself and enter the parlour, which once formed a section of a separate building, occupied after her marriage by Joan Hart and family. The parlour would have been a general purpose room and used as a bedchamber as necessary, and is decorated with brightly painted cloths – often used to reduce draughts as well as for decoration. Noticeable is the old flooring of broken flag stones. There is a bed which came from Anne Hathaway's Cottage (D6) and is a copy of a rare 16th century type, with bed hangings of woven curtains featuring a colour and design of the Elizabethan period.

The hall was the main room of the house and was used for dining purposes. An original fireplace has a spit for roasting meat and a range of cooking utensils. There is a replica hanging cupboard, a gothic-style stool and a bench. Beyond the hall is a cross-passage, which led to the house's original doorway on Henley Street. On the far side of the passage is a room thought to have been John Shakespeare's workshop, which features displays of 16th century glove making, tanning and wool processing.

On reaching the upper level we find three rooms once used as bedchambers. In the first is a bed with hangings of 16th century design, based on a wall-painting. The second is more of an exhibition room and explains something of the history of the Birthplace, including its development into a literary shrine. Of special significance is a former window, transferred from the third bedroom – the room in which Will is thought to have been born. Many notables of the 19th century etched their names on the glass panes – people such as Thomas Carlyle, Sir Walter Scott, Charles Dickens, John Keats, Lord Tennyson, Henry Longfellow, Thomas Hardy, Mark Twain, Harriet Beecher Stowe, and Sir Henry Irving. Patronage of the Birthplace goes back to the mid-18th century.

The third bedchamber (directly over the parlour, with a low ceiling) is entered. It is, by tradition, the actual room in which William Shakespeare was born, though there can be no definite proof. Again, the red and green bed hangings and floral wall decor are copied from 16th century patterning. Many visitors are intrigued by the replica of a small truckle bed which neatly hides away under the main bed. It is mounted on a set of wheels and was often used by children or servants.

Noticeable on each side of the bed are pairs of staves or staffes – contraptions for holding bedclothes in place. This type of bed would normally have been kept in the parents' bedchamber. Other artifacts in the room include a family Bible, a rocking cradle, a wicker basket for laundry, a wash tub, toys and baby clothes. All of these are copies of objects made in Shakespeare's time.

Moving into the rear wing, probably added when the house was used as an inn, take note of the original staircase, then enter the two former bedchambers. The rear room contains an interpretive display chart tracing the ownership of the house from John Shakespeare onwards (it includes two former signs from the Swan and Maidenhead Inn). It is thought the second room was built shortly after the death of John in 1601, in readiness for the house being turned into a public hostelry.

Descending to ground level again, we enter a room of longer proportions, dating from the 17th century. It was used as the kitchen and the adjoining buttery was used for curing and food storage. As one might expect, exhibition displays in both rooms deal with domestic chores and cookery, and include items such as pewter eating and drinking utensils, kitchen furniture and samples of original ceramic and earthenware objects. Especially inviting in the kitchen is the open hearth feature, the warmest place in many households, which includes an iron fire basket for coal. In winter, the family would often eat their meals in this area as it was much warmer than the rest of the house.

After a short stroll around the rear garden – planted with many of the trees, flowers and herbs mentioned in Shakespeare's works (during the summer the paths abound with bright yellow verbascums and tall hollyhocks) – take a last look at the Birthplace, which has become an integral part of Britain's heritage. As well as acting as a magnet for many famous people it became the centrepiece for the town's first Shakespeare festival, held in 1769, which was organised by distinguished Lichfield-born actor, David Garrick (1717–79). Thereafter, visitors came in their droves to see the Birthplace and, unfortunately, souvenir hunters soon began to hack away at the poet's famous chair, selling pieces to an adoring public desperate for all things Shakespearean. The house was eventually put up for auction following the death of its last occupier, Mrs Court. On 16 September 1847, the building was purchased for £3,000 from monies raised by public subscription. This was the forerunner of the Birthplace Trust.

After an almost complete change of its outward appearance during the 19th century, the house was acquired by the Trust in 1891 and restoration work began. In general, the house retains the likeness and character that appear in the earliest drawing of it, made by Richard Greene of Lichfield in 1769. In the time of Shakespeare it formed part of a continuous frontage of houses, but today stands free of adjoining buildings. With the part pedestrianisation of Henley Street over recent years, the appearance of the Birthplace has been much enhanced, as it is mostly free of the passing traffic and parked vehicles that clutter the other parts of the busy town centre.

Adjacent to the Birthplace and overlooking its rear garden is the modern Shakespeare Centre, the administrative home of the Birthplace Trust, set up to maintain the properties associated with Shakespeare and to advance knowledge of the Bard, his work, and the age he lived in. It houses a library, study centre, and archive of local history.

I wasted time, and now doth time waste me

Richard II, Act 5, Scene 5

The three shifts in England's religion within the space of about twenty four years brought about disruption, misunderstanding and chaos amongst the various practitioners. Change was more evident in the larger cities than in smaller places such as Stratford, where movement away from old practices was very slow. After all, both the Shakespeare and Arden families came from country yeomen stock in the Forest of Arden where, for centuries, time had stood still.

For some people the change back to the Protestant faith provided new opportunities and John Shakespeare was an ambitious man eager to move up in the world and become a member of the new Tudor middle-class. One way of achieving his goal was to join the local civic order. He therefore got elected as one of the fourteen Capital Burgesses who, together with fourteen Aldermen, comprised the Corporation of Stratford under the chairmanship of the Bailiff. On 4 July 1565 he became an alderman, taking an oath to see to the welfare of the townsfolk of Stratford. In 1568 he was elected Bailiff (or mayor) of Stratford, the town's chief officer. One of his responsibilities was to act as local agent to the government in London. Yet John is thought to still have had leanings toward the Catholic faith and it must have been a bitter pill to swallow, accepting the new ways of the Elizabethan court. It meant going against both his long-held principles and, indeed, some of his long-standing friends in the town.

During his time as Bailiff, John Shakespeare officially entertained a distinguished group of actors. It was the first time in the history of the town that such an honour had been extended. These actors were members of two separate companies: the Queen's Men and the Earl of Leicester's Men. Both played in Stratford on several occasions. In 1574, Queen Elizabeth issued the first known performance license to the Earl of Leicester's troupe (to prevent their arrest as 'vagabonds'). Among them was the businessman James Burbage. The Queen's Men were paid nine shillings by John Shakespeare on behalf of the town, and Earl of Leicester's Men only twelve pence. No doubt seeing these players perform had a far-reaching effect on the young Will which might well have whetted his appetite for a future life in the theatre.

The Guild Chapel, Stratford

Further details – Tel: 0870 160 7930 – Stratford TIC

Local councillors were ordered by the Government to desecrate all images which suggested any form of Popery or old superstitions. The

The Guild Chapel

Guild Chapel in Stratford was a prime target as it contained some elaborate medieval religious wall paintings. John Shakespeare, while serving as Bailiff in 1563, was given responsibility of supervising the defacement of these decorations. These included pictures of Heaven and Hell; St George and the Dragon; the murder of Thomas à Becket; two Saxon saints, Edmund and Modwena; and, over the great arch leading to the chancel, the Last Judgement. As very few worshippers were able to read, the visual impact of these paintings conveyed a story to them about the doctrines and teaching of the Roman Catholic Church. Rather than eliminate them altogether, the councillors made a shrewd move by covering them with just one coat of whitewash. The paintings were finally uncovered in 1804 but some did not survive renovations to the Chapel undertaken in that year. Several others were lost in 1835, when a gallery was erected at the west end of the nave.

The building also has some modern stained glass windows depicting famous people connected with the town's history – Robert de Stratford,

founder of the Guild; Sir Hugh Clopton; Thomas Jolyffe, benefactor
of the local grammar school; John Shakespeare; and others. The Guild
Chapel is situated on the corner of Chapel Lane and Church Street,
overlooking New Place and opposite the half-timbered frontage of the
Falcon Hotel. By 1269, the Guild of the Holy Cross was already in
existence. Parts of the original building were incorporated into a largely
re-built chapel during the 15th century, including a nave and west
tower, the latter having been paid for by Sir Hugh Clopton. It was a
regular place of worship and a meeting centre for Guild members,
who gained a growing influence in the running of local affairs.

The Guild Chapel has, over the years, played a central part in the
life of the Stratford community. It has also served as a chapel for the
nearby grammar school and Shakespeare would have known it well.

King Edward VI Grammar School and Guildhall, Stratford

Further details – Tel: 0870 160 7930 – Stratford TIC

Adjoining the Guild Chapel on Church Lane is an excellent example
of a long range of half-timbered buildings comprising the Guildhall,
grammar school and some attractive almshouses (C9). The grammar
school can trace its origins back to 1295, when there was an entry made
in the records of the Bishop of Worcester of the ordination of two deacons
– William Grenefeld, rector of the church of Stratford-upon-Avon,
and Richard, *rector scolarum*. They would have been employed by the
local Guild soon after its foundation. It was well established by the 15th
century and one of the Guild's priests, Thomas Jolyffe, first endowed
the school in 1482. Earlier, in 1427, the timber-framed school house was
built and named Pedagogue's House – it is thought to be the oldest
school building in the country still in use. Fortunately, many records have
survived which document the school's early history. Even though the
Guild's possessions were claimed by the Crown at the Reformation,
the school was re-founded in 1553 by Edward VI who, when granting
a charter of incorporation to the Borough of Stratford-upon-Avon,
charged the Corporation with the responsibility of maintaining the
almshouses and the school. It was named King Edward VI School in
his honour and the Upper Guildhall became the town's schoolroom.

It was to this grammar school that one can assume the seven-year-
old William Shakespeare was sent about 1571, having received an

informal education from his mother at their Henley Street home. Education was free up to the age of sixteen for the sons of burgesses. However, part of the qualification for entrance was that each boy be able to read and write basic English and, preferably, have some initial knowledge of Latin. The Guildhall was erected in 1417-18 and the local council usually met on the ground floor of the building. The school library now occupies this room, in which some interesting and original wall paintings have recently been uncovered. After early training, scholars moved into the 'big' school section where, for centuries, schoolboys were taught the rudiments of Greek grammar and Latin (this room is still used for Junior Assemblies and teaching purposes).

The room is presided over by the Headmaster's chair and high on the west wall is mounted a large wooden board containing the names of each schoolmaster since the school was re-founded. It shows that between 1571–75 the office was held by Simon Hunt, who also held the curacy of the nearby village of Luddington. He was succeeded by Thomas Jenkins, who was probably Shakespeare's principal teacher for the remainder of his schooldays. This man is thought to have been the model for Sir Hugh Evans, an academic depicted in Act 4, Scene 1 of *The Merry Wives Of Windsor*. The schoolmaster received an income of £20 per year from the local council, and a house and removal expenses when first appointed. Schoolmasters were educated at Oxford and usually had a strong Roman Catholic background. In Will's day the whole school of forty pupils was taught in the Upper Guildhall and the half-timbered room remains little altered apart from the desks, which only go back 200 years. Desks and forms were so arranged as to face one another along the sides of the room, which remained the 'big' school's sole place of teaching until the 1880s. Adjacent is what is known as The Council Chamber, once used by Guild priests. It contains a Jacobean council table which has been desecrated over the years by hundreds of scholars, who have left their names or initials indented into its surface. The table was bequeathed to the School when the Corporation finally moved out of the building in the late 19th century. Ancient paintings of roses occupy the wall opposite the window. The room is still in use for meetings and teaching purposes.

The whole complex of buildings – the Guild Chapel, Guildhall and almshouses – is an architectural gem. However, only the Guild Chapel is open to the public on a daily basis. To view the interior of the school (groups only), special permission has to be obtained in advance from the Headmaster. Visits are only permitted during Easter and summer holidays.

Rather like matters of state and religion, education was in something of a turmoil in Shakespeare's day. New schools were fast appearing across the country (160 were founded during the reign of Elizabeth I) and young men were emerging from them far better educated and more literate than their forebears. They were producing a fine new class of gentlemen who would use their knowledge and talents for the betterment of the nascent Tudor era. Hours at grammar school were long and pupils were expected to work six days a week, with breakfast at six o'clock in the morning and lessons continuing for about eleven hours, with only a short break for lunch.

The required language for teaching was Latin, which must have been spoken by Will from the age of eight upwards. Other subjects would have included Greek, a little Hebrew and some of the classics. He would have read the tragedies of Seneca and the comedies of Plautus. Reading the works of such literary greats proved invaluable to the young lad and he would often recall them in later life. Shakespeare was especially fond of Greek dramas and the history of the Roman Empire. One has only to think of his Roman plays such as *Anthony and Cleopatra, Coriolanus* and *Julius Caesar* to see how his passion for the subject was to influence his writings. Another book with which Will would have been very familiar was the Bible. It is possible he used a number of biblical themes as background plots. For instance, he mentions the story of Cain and Abel on numerous occasions in his plays. There was schooling in the art of debating, persuasive speech and writing – essential attributes for any student or would-be writer – plus straightforward commonsense and logic.

On the ground floor, until the suppression of the Guilds, the Guildhall was a venue for a Tudor ceremony called the Annual Guild Feast. There were displays of music, dancing, songs, ballads, mime and other theatrical performances, put on by teams of strolling players who moved from town to town providing entertainment. Part of the repertoire included plays and recitals of classical works, as well as some bawdy comedies. Will's young appetite for drama and romance could well have been further fuelled with an early glimpse of the actor's lifestyle. Such boyhood dreams!

... with his satchel
and shining morning face, creeping like snail
unwillingly to school

As You Like It, Act 2, Scene 7

Touring players and entertainers also performed in taverns, any available hall, and out of door locations such as open markets, streets and the ground in front of public buildings. Sometimes their performances included mystery plays which, in the main, were re-enactments of Biblical stories. The ancient city of Coventry, 18 miles (29km) from Stratford and the third largest settlement in England, had a tradition of performing a famous cycle of mystery plays every year, eventually suppressed by Anglican Church authorities as being 'too Catholic'. The Coventry Players are known to have performed at Bristol in 1570, and the town of Stratford was en route. It is therefore highly probable they stopped off to perform there and John Shakespeare may well have taken his eldest son along to see them on such an occasion.

Each troupe of players had to obtain a venue licence to stage their plays at the various towns where they toured and, in Stratford-upon-Avon, this would have been from the Guildhall, through its bailiff, the man charged with issuing such warrants. As John Shakespeare held this office for a time, he would most certainly have met the visiting groups. This again would have brought Will in close proximity with such companies of actors.

It is also most probable that in 1575, at the age of eleven, Will was taken to Kenilworth, 12 miles (10km) from his home town. He would have witnessed a dazzling programme of medieval jousting, pageants, musical entertainment, theatrical events and fireworks. The reason for the celebration was the last of four visits made to Kenilworth Castle by Queen Elizabeth, who stayed there for nineteen days. Earlier, in 1563, the Queen handed the castle to Robert Dudley as a gift, a year before creating him Earl of Leicester. In August 1566, she spent a few days with Leicester at Kenilworth, calling on his brother, the Earl of Warwick, at Warwick Castle, and also at Charlecote, Sir Thomas Lucy's recently rebuilt house near Stratford. Leicester had become Elizabeth's court favourite and was undoubtedly anxious to show his gratitude to his Sovereign by putting on a lavish programme of entertainment. Surely she could not have failed to have been impressed by such hospitality?

Kenilworth Castle (EH)

Tel: 01926 852078

Some years after the Norman conquest, King Henry I gave the royal estate of Stoneleigh (D15), which included Kenilworth, to his Treasurer, Geoffrey de Clinton. In turn, de Clinton built, in 1122, the first castle, of timber construction, and also founded a nearby priory and granted it to some Augustinian Canons. De Clinton later rebuilt the castle in stone on a more ambitious scale during the reign of Henry II and included a large keep. In the reign of King John the castle reverted to the Crown, continuing until 1264. In that year it was handed to Simon de Montfort, Earl of Leicester, whose wife was the sister of Henry III. Kenilworth became de Montfort's power base during the Barons' War, in his struggle against his brother-in-law, the King. Henry III besieged the castle in 1266 after de Montfort had rebelled against him, and eventually starved the defenders into surrender. This is known as the Siege of Kenilworth.

In the 14th century the castle was enlarged and converted into a palace by John of Gaunt, son of Edward III. He built a great hall – said to be the finest in the land apart from Westminster – and other facilities, in the ward inside the original curtain wall. The palace stayed in Crown possession until it was given by Queen Elizabeth to Robert Dudley, who erected new properties, including Leicester's Building and the Gatehouse, to both impress and entertain his Sovereign. After Dudley's death in 1588, Kenilworth Castle was re-claimed by the Crown and then sold in 1611 at a knock-down price. Fifteen years later it became part of the French Queen Henrietta Maria's marriage portion – she was the wife of Charles I. Sadly, Kenilworth was bombarded and captured by Parliamentary forces during the Civil War. Since the 17th century the castle has been mostly unoccupied but, though mainly ruinous, substantial parts of the great fortified palace still survive. They include the 12th century keep, the unroofed Great Hall built for John of Gaunt, Leicester's Building, and the 16th century Gatehouse.

The site was later immortalized by Sir Walter Scott in his book *Kenilworth* – one of the *Waverley* novels – which he set in Elizabethan times, when the castle was in its heyday.

Brevity is the soul of wit

Hamlet, Act 2, Scene 2

John Shakespeare continued to thrive both as a civic official and businessman until the mid-1570s and, to enhance and secure his position, he even applied to the College of Arms to obtain his own coat of arms. It was refused and, for some reason, the matter wasn't pursued until much later, by Will, who successfully canvassed on his father's behalf.

John fell from grace as a member of the town council when some underhand and illegal dealings in the wool trade, termed as 'brogging,' were uncovered. His misdemeanours could have brought about a spell in prison but, fortunately for him, he escaped with a fine. He also failed to appear at the town council meeting or any other meetings during 1577 or the following year. (It was also in 1577 that Francis Drake set off on a voyage that would take him round the world.)

To make matters worse, there was an economic slump in the wool trade which almost drove John to bankruptcy. So there was no way he could have continued the mode of living to which he had become accustomed over previous years. The outlook was far from rosy.

As the years went by, John Shakespeare's business dealings deteriorated, which meant – when the time came – he could not afford to send his son to university. His fall from favour also meant his resignation, or exclusion, from his position at the local Corporation. This had a direct repercussion on Will, who was probably around sixteen years of age when he was compelled to leave grammar school. Nevertheless, the lad had already received a sound schooling in history and the classics, which had been well and truly instilled in his creative mind. Unfortunately, no school records exist from that time so it is impossible to state his actual date of departure.

The knowledge that William Shakespeare gleaned from his grammar school days, and the geographical environment of his boyhood and youth, were to play important roles in the shaping of his future life and writings.

How many goodly creatures are there here!
How beauteous mankind is! O brave new world
that has such people in't!

The Tempest, Act 5, Scene 1

CHAPTER 3

Religious Unrest

DURING THE LATTER half of the 1570s, Queen Elizabeth's commissioners decided on a purge of those who were still maintaining Roman Catholic practices in England – and there were many. Stratford-upon-Avon harboured plenty such people and in late 1576 government forces arrived under the command of an official enforcer, Sir Thomas Lucy of Charlecote, a member of the local gentry loyal to Queen Elizabeth. Bishops were instructed to report anyone refusing to attend Protestant church services and to submit a summary of their assets to government authorities. At the beginning of 1578, Aldermen in Stratford were presented with a levy to assist in enlarging forces to quell the anti-Protestant feelings. John Shakespeare was among them and though he was asked to pay the levy, he bluntly refused. Shortly afterwards, due to failing business deals, John started to sell off some of his assets in land and property.

Undoubtedly, Elizabeth I was nervous of her position on the throne. To Catholics she would always remain illegitimate because of her parents' so-called 'bigamous' marriage. In Catholic eyes, the rightful claimant to the throne of England was Mary Queen of Scots, who was a direct descendant of Henry VIII's elder sister, Margaret Tudor. Margaret was her maternal grandmother. The Scottish Queen became an obvious champion not only for English Catholics but for those in countries such as Spain and France and, of course, the papal authorities. The possibility of invasion from the continent was ever looming, threatening Elizabeth's position.

By the spring of 1580 rumours reached court that, besides a planned landing in Ireland by English Catholics, Jesuit priests from the continent were to infiltrate local communities across England to generate a Roman Catholic revival. These rumours were not unfounded and in the following June the man selected to lead the Jesuit mission, Edmund Campion – a former Oxford scholar and recusant – arrived at the port of Dover (B7). (Many Jesuits were recruited from Oxford (B17) and Cambridge (E23) universities and sent to various seminaries in Rome, Douai and Rheims to receive training as priests). But Elizabeth's spy network had not been idle and Campion was arrested for interrogation as soon as his ship landed in Dover. Though cross-examined by the local mayor, he was released from detention. A lucky escape! He made his way to London and was given shelter by Catholic sympathisers in the borough of Southwark. It was there he laid plans and plotted his spiritual revolution to revitalise Catholicism. Other Jesuits who landed in England were not quite so fortunate as Campion and one was arrested for what was considered by the authorities to be 'bringing in subversive printed material' which promoted the papal religion.

Both the Shakespeares and the Ardens had relatives who were involved, or had close links, with Jesuits. When William Shakespeare started at King Edward VI Grammar School in Stratford his master was Simon Hunt, who later left to become a Jesuit priest. Hunt accompanied Robert Debdale of nearby Shottery (D6), a relative of Mary Shakespeare. There was also Thomas Cottom, brother to John Cottom, later master at the grammar school; and Robert Persons, a friend of another of Mary's relatives, Edward Arden. Debdale, Cottom and Persons met up with Campion in London to discuss matters of strategy on maintaining and spreading the Catholic tradition. Afterwards, they went their separate ways to various counties to pursue their individual missions.

Robert Persons headed for the Stratford area, where there was known support amongst the local community. Most families around the town were Catholic sympathisers, including the Ardens, Cloptons, Catesbys and Throckmortons, and each could most probably be relied upon to assist or support him in some way. A particular 'safe house' for meetings by recusants and Jesuits was Baddesley Clinton, which was owned by the Ferrers family.

Baddesley Clinton (NT)

Tel: 01564 783294

Baddesley Clinton is situated some seven miles (11km) north west of Warwick, just off the A41. It is a moated manor house of stone, brick and some half-timbering and dates from 1300. The buildings stand on three sides of a quadrangle, the stone front facing north east, with a tower entrance approached by a small Queen Anne brick bridge over the moat. These features, together with tall decorative chimneys and a gateway with an embattled porch higher than the roof, give the place a romantic atmosphere. The front, north wing dates from the mid or late 15th century, part of the work of John Brome and his son Nicholas, who died in 1517. From Nicholas's daughter the property and estate passed in 1517 to her husband, Sir Edward Ferrers, and the building remained in the Ferrers family in direct descent until 1884. This wing includes the library, great parlour, a secret room with access to the moat, and two bedrooms above the drawing and dining rooms, containing 16th or 17th century paneling and carved fireplaces. The south east wing of external 18th century brick and half timbered gables dates from the late 16th century. Contained here is the Great Hall with a finely carved heraldic stone fireplace. Finally, the south west wing at the rear includes an added inner wing built in Victorian times, containing the Chapel, kitchens and bedrooms.

Most of the handiwork is that of Henry Ferrers, an antiquarian, whose life spanned 1549–1633 and who was known to William Shakespeare. It was he who was responsible for altering and up-grading the house. He also constructed the Great Hall in the 1580s and filled the house with ornate chimney pieces, decorative paneling and heraldic glass, some of which dates from 1560. It has been little changed since his death. The interiors today reflect the house's heyday in the Elizabethan period, when it became a haven for persecuted Catholics and had no fewer than three priest holes where they could hide.

The house was taken over by the National Trust in the 1980s and is open to the public. The Ferrers family and others connected with Baddesley Clinton are commemorated in the nearby Church of St Michael, situated 250 yards (229m) from the house. It is mainly Perpendicular and has a tower donated by Nicholas Brome.

Packwood House (NT)

Tel: 01564 783294

Whilst in the area of Baddesley Clinton, it is well worth making the journey to Packwood House, just 2 miles (3.2km) further along Rising Lane (follow signposts). It dates from the 16th century and has a history of royal connections. For instance, the future Charles II was given refreshment there after his defeat at the Battle of Worcester (D1) in 1651. It has lavish interiors with French and Flemish tapestries and furniture from the 17th and 18th centuries. Outside are some wonderful herbaceous borders and gardens, together with topiary of yew trees said to represent the Sermon on the Mount.

Of local interest is an ornate fireplace and over mantle, dated 1595, which originated in Stratford and is now set in the great hall of Packwood House. It was once rescued from a fire at the home of the wine merchant John Smith and his wife, who lived at 35 High Street in

Stratford. The remaining contents of their house were sold at auction, held by a man called Oliver Baker, a well-known art dealer and antiquarian in the Stratford area. The unit was later acquired for Packwood House.

Before long, court officials became aware of the movements and scheming of the Jesuits and, despite their efforts, they were rounded up. Robert Debdale was first to be arrested, then Thomas Cottom. Robert Persons managed to get back to France, while Edmund Campion was at large for at least a year before he was finally discovered after a major manhunt. In the meanwhile, he spent some time in the Chilterns and at Hoghton Tower (E4) and Lea Hall, both in Lancashire, as guest of Alexander Hoghton, an ardent Catholic.

The trials of Campion and Cottom took place in London during November 1581 but the outcome was a foregone conclusion. They were hung, drawn and quartered at Tyburn (A15), the traditional place of execution in days gone by for highwaymen, criminals and others who flouted English law. It is close to the area of the present Marble Arch.

Many years later, in 1757, an interesting discovery was made by workmen in the eaves of the Shakespeare Birthplace in Henley Street. It was a document of six pages, hand written in English, each page being signed in the name of one John Shakespeare. It was what was thought to be a Catholic 'testament of faith' which not only professed complete allegiance to the Roman Church but also that John would instruct his relatives and close friends to hold Catholic masses to pray for his soul after death. These were the sorts of commitment that Jesuit priests had been aiming to encourage throughout their 1580 mission. So, despite earlier promises as a Stratford town councillor to uphold the religion and sovereignty of Queen Elizabeth, John Shakespeare was in secret still wholly committed to the Catholic faith. Knowledge of this by other persons would most certainly not have helped his case and could well have speeded his downfall. That he successfully managed to retain his business probably indicates that, although not attending Anglican church services in case he was spotted by creditors, he still appeared publicly to retain his loyalty to the Crown. He was skating on very thin ice and most probably attended secret Catholic masses and services in the private homes of other local recusants. It was a dangerous life to pursue and John Shakespeare must have been always in fear of discovery.

The devil can cite Scripture for his purpose

The Merchant of Venice, Act 1, Scene 3

CHAPTER 4

The 'Lost' Years

THERE HAS BEEN much speculation as to what Will Shakespeare did from when he left grammar school until the time he was appearing as an actor and playwright in London. Unfortunately, no specific records exist to throw light upon the subject. He possibly began working as an assistant in his father's trade as a glove maker at their Henley Street home. Over the years, various theories have been introduced by authors and experts in the field of all things Shakespearean. The simple fact is that there is no definite proof for any one of them.

National celebrations took place in September 1580 when Francis Drake arrived back in Plymouth after his circumnavigation of the world. He continued his voyage along the South Coast and into the Thames Estuary, arriving at Greenwich (B9) on 4 April 1581. It was there that Queen Elizabeth gave a lavish banquet in his honour on board ship and knighted him Sir Francis. He was not only the first Englishmen to sail around the globe but also the first to found a colony on the eastern side of the North American continent, naming it 'Virginia' after his Queen.

Things went from bad to worse in the Shakespeare household due to John's declining business and social status. There was also a disastrous winter in 1578 when many people in Stratford were taken ill. Amongst the casualties was Will's sister, Anne, who died at the age of four years and was buried at Holy Trinity Church on 4 April 1579. Despite the sadness, having a growing family to clothe and feed, John and Mary probably both felt it was vital that young Will should play his part in supplementing the family income. He most likely left grammar school at around the age of fifteen, as his father's financial and social decline would have prevented him from going on to Oxford to continue his education. For the time being, his efforts would be needed in the family business.

However, one of the most plausible of cases – and a theory put forward over recent years by a number of people in the north of England – is that Will went away to work as a schoolmaster and player for a wealthy Catholic landowner, Alexander Hoghton, at a house called Hoghton Tower near Blackburn in Lancashire. It is an avenue we might do well to explore.

In upper class families it was the norm to employ a tutor or schoolmaster to educate the children. In general, girls were taught music whilst boys concentrated on grammar and arithmetic. English law at that time prevented the employment of such posts unless specifically approved by an Anglican bishop, but there was a means of avoiding the problem, especially amongst Catholic families, by describing the tutor as a 'servant'.

Though John Shakespeare was the family figurehead, it was his wife, Mary, who was considered to have the wider influence – especially in Catholic circles – and she was ambitious for her son to succeed, instead of following in his father's footsteps as a small town merchant. No doubt she encouraged her husband to find a suitable post for Will. Both parents knew the Stratford schoolmaster, John Cottom – another secretly practicing Catholic, the brother of the ill-fated Jesuit priest, Thomas Cottom. John Cottom was from Tarnacre (E3), close to Cottom Hall near Preston, Lancashire. A nearby neighbour was Alexander Hoghton, a member of a powerful Catholic family, who was seeking a tutor for his children. The theory is that after some discussion with the Shakespeares, Cottom returned to Lancashire, taking Will with him to commence the post. Alexander Hoghton happened to employ a group of theatrical players.

The Hoghtons were wealthy landowners with many properties, the principal ones being Hoghton Tower and Lea Hall (now a farm called Lea Old Hall), which are about twelve miles (19km) apart. The family fortunes had improved in the 14th century by the marriage of Sir Richard de Hoghton and Sybilla de Lea from Lea Hall. In Shakespeare's youth, the head of the family was Thomas Hoghton (1518–1580), who rebuilt Hoghton Tower between 1560–65. He was unable to accept the religious and political changes brought about by Elizabeth's reign and became a recusant. This gentleman was closely acquainted with important but dangerous friends who also supported the old religion. One of his closest allies was Cardinal Allen from the nearby manor of Rossall. Rather than continue living under a Protestant queen, Thomas Hoghton decided upon exile in the Spanish Netherlands, where he died at an English seminary at Douai. He left the running of his properties and estates to his half-brother Richard at Park Hall, but Alexander, his full brother, was named as legal heir, though he survived Thomas by just one year.

The Jesuit priest, Edmund Campion, also stayed at Hoghton Tower around Easter 1581 and, whilst there, left some secret documents for safe keeping. Jesuit priests were able to lie low in priest holes and thus avoid capture by Government troops and officials, and Hoghton Tower had plenty such hiding places.

Hoghton Tower
Tel: 01254 852 986

Hoghton Tower has hitherto been most famous as the location where King James I knighted a loin of beef 'Sir Loin' in 1617. It is a fortified 16th century manor house built on a hilltop near Blackburn. Important guests have included William III, George V and Queen Mary, but the thought that William Shakespeare may have begun his working life here is arousing much curiosity. The house sits in a commanding position at the tip of the Pendle range of hills, midway between Preston and Blackburn, and is reached by a long narrow drive of over half a mile. In Saxon and Norman times the de Hoghton family lived at the foot of the hill beside the River Darwen.

On reaching the hall from the drive, the visitor passes through a perimeter wall onto the tilting green, an open space once used for jousting and other such events, which has a fine set of 18th century piers (platforms used for staging entertainment). The large gatehouse leads to the outer courtyard, a general purpose area which includes a south wing, once a farm building, and a north wing where the servants lived and worked. Some steps lead up to an arch, through which the upper and inner courtyards can be reached. It was above this archway that the great keep once towered, but it was blown up during the Civil Wars in 1642 and was never rebuilt.

The courtyard was at the centre of the de Hoghtons' private apartments, with steps on the northern side leading to the fine banqueting hall. Through the west door is the oak parlour, with lovely decorations and panelling. Here the visitor finds an elegant and spacious staircase to the upper chamber and a suite of rooms. These include a 'State Bedroom', 'King's Ante Chamber', 'Guinea Room' and 'Buckingham Room' (named after George Villiers, Duke of Buckingham, who accompanied King James I on his visit to Hoghton in 1617). There is also a 'Bed Chamber' where, according to tradition, the King ordered his bed to be placed when he stayed. From the upper chamber visitors are directed along the King's Hall to the chapel entrance. The hall bears the royal coat of arms which records the visit by King George V and Queen Mary in 1913.

The banqueting hall is perhaps the place of most interest to visitors as, if the 'tutor' theory is correct, it was here that the young William Shakespeare would have enjoyed performances by Alexander Hoghton's troupe of players. It was here also that King James 1 knighted 'Sir Loin'. Beyond is a ladies' withdrawing room, where they retired while gentlemen followed their own pursuits.

The visitor passes by the great kitchens and ancillary rooms and an intriguing priest hole. As you depart, you pass an old well-house with early Tudor wooden wheels, and can gaze into the deep well before taking your leave through the gatehouse arch. Hopefully you will be able to enjoy the panoramic views afforded on clear days as far as the Lake District, the Irish Sea, extensive parts of Lancashire and – with a good pair of binoculars – the mountains of the Snowdon range in North Wales.

The robb'd that smiles steals something from the thief

Othello, Act 1, Scene 3

It is Alexander Houghton's will which has given rise to speculation over whether William Shakespeare might have worked in Lancashire. The will contains the following section:

> *It is my mind and will that the said Thomas Hoghton my brother shall have all my instruments belonging to musics and all manner of play clothes if he be minded to keep and do keep his players. And if he will not keep and maintain players, then it is my mind that Sir Thomas Hesketh, knight, shall have the same instruments and play clothes. And I most heartedly require the said Sir Thomas to be friendly unto Fulk Gillom and William Shakeshafte now dwelling with me and either take them into his service or else help them to some good master as my trust is he will.*

Sir Thomas Hesketh (1539–88) lived at his ancestral home, Rufford Old Hall (E5), near Ormskirk, and succeeded his father, Sir Robert, as Lord of the Manor in 1539.

Rufford Old Hall (NT)

Tel: 01704 821254

The house, which stands among trees a little to the north of the village of Rufforth, is believed to have been built in the early 15th century by another Sir Thomas Hesketh, replacing an older building. Sir Thomas held the manor between 1416 and 1458. The house comprises the original great hall, of timber construction, a wing in brick built in 1662, and an intervening section which dates mostly from 1821. The half-timbered house follows a typical medieval plan, comprising an east and a west wing joined to a central hall. The impressive great hall remains practically unaltered and has an intricately carved wooden screen and dramatic hammer-beam roof. Evidence suggests that Shakespeare may have performed in this hall for Sir Thomas, whose family owned Rufford for over 400 years. The house contains fine collections of 16th and 17th century oak furniture, arms, armour and tapestries. The grounds are laid out in Victorian style and feature a herbaceous border, an orchard, topiary and sculpture. When the west gable was rebuilt in 1949 a secret chamber was revealed and it was found that the decorative features of the roof were continued behind the canopy, while its rafters extended down to the eaves and ended underneath the roof of the bay. The chamber may have been constructed during the religious strife in the second half of the 16th century.

It was in 1581 that Sir Thomas was requested, under the terms of Alexander Hoghton's will, to accept 'instruments and playclothes' (from either of his halls), and to take 'Fulk Gillom and William Shakeshafte' onto his staff, or to find them alternative employment. (In those days, it was common that a surname's spelling could include a number of variations. Both William Shakespeare's father and grandfather were guilty of signing their names in a variety of styles.) If we are right to assume that William Shakeshafte and William Shakespeare are one and the same person, it would mean he had already been employed by the Hoghton family as part of a group of players. The argument against this theory is that there were many people called Shakeshafte already in Lancashire and it could have been any one of them. The fact of the matter is that the subject is still open to debate, until such time as more positive documentation comes to light either to support the argument or to place Shakespeare elsewhere.

At the time of Alexander Houghton's death, Sir Thomas Hesketh was in Lancaster Castle gaol (E2) for recusancy. In his absence, some claim that Shakeshafte was nevertheless accepted into the household at Rufford but this is uncertain. Well-to-do families often employed a band of players or performers for their own entertainment and that of their guests. Another nearby household who could afford to do so was that of Henry, 4th Earl of Derby and his son, Ferdinando Stanley, Lord

Strange, who kept players at Knowsley (E6) and Lathom. The pair lived about ten miles (16km) from Sir Thomas Hesketh. It was to them that Sir Thomas was reputed to have passed Shakeshafte under the clause of Alexander Houghton's will.

For Will it would have been a good move as the Stanleys were far more influential than Houghton or Hesketh and were well-known for their hospitality to struggling players and poets. Ferdinando controlled his own company, known as Lord Strange's Men, and they regularly toured and performed in different towns and venues. Lord Derby had a troupe which had a fine reputation and attracted audiences from a wide area. On one occasion it was recorded that the Earl of Leicester's Men had performed alongside those of Sir Thomas Hesketh at Lathom Castle and Knowsley. To someone like William Shakeshafte, whether or not he was our man from Stratford, it would have presented another opportunity for making good contacts and learning something of the actor's craft. Inevitably it would have helped foster the enthusiasm for all things theatrical which, if he was in fact Shakespeare, was to develop so brilliantly in a few years time. Will was to work with Ferdinando again in London.

He draweth out the thread of his verbosity finer than the staple of his argument

Love's Labour Lost, Act 5, Scene 1

Even if the theory that Will spent some time in Lancashire is correct, it is nonetheless not known just how long he stayed there or whether he made any visits back home to see his family. However, what is known for certain is that he was around Stratford just prior to and during 1582, when he made his future wife pregnant. He married, at the age of eighteen, Anne Hathaway, from the nearby hamlet of Shottery, a short walking distance from Stratford. She was eight years his senior. No doubt young Will had been sowing his wild oats, with the result that a shotgun wedding took place to retain some measure of respectability in a strongly religious community. Will was still considered a minor and would have had to obtain his parents' permission to wed. A special license had first to be granted by the Bishop of Worcester's ecclesiastical court as, due to the urgency of the marriage, there was no time for the usual banns to be proclaimed. This entailed a trip to the city of Worcester to obtain appropriate documentation.

By tradition, Will set off from Stratford to Worcester accompanied by two local farmers from Shottery – Fulk Sandells and John Richardson – friends of Anne's father, Richard Hathaway. Perhaps they accompanied the lad to ensure he did the right thing by their colleague's pregnant daughter? It is thought they stayed overnight at the Bull Inn at the village of Inkberrow (D2), about half way between the two centres, and it is probable they spent the evening drinking before resuming their journey on the morrow. (The surrounding areas of Inkberrow and Hanbury have found fame over recent years as the bases for the fictional community in the long-running BBC radio saga *The Archers*. The programme started on 1 January 1951 and the fictional Ambridge, in and around which the serial is set, is a composite of the local villages. The Bull pub, where so much village life is centred, is thought to be modeled on the fine timber-framed inn where Shakespeare once stayed.)

In Shakespeare's time a marriage certificate as we know it did not exist and, in the circumstances surrounding his marriage, it was necessary to get official sanction to depart from normal requirements. This took the form of a *licence*. Licences were not uncommon – the consistory court of the Bishop of Worcester, which undertook such matters, issued 98 in 1582, the year Shakespeare obtained his. To obtain a licence the applicant required other documents – an *allegation*, giving details of the parties and their parents or guardians, as well as the reason for the dispensation; a *certificate* from the parents or guardians asserting that there was no objection to the marriage; and a *bond* to ensure the bishop and his officers should not suffer from any legal action arising out of the grant of the licence. A fee was paid, and the issue of the licence was recorded in the bishop's register.

In the case of William Shakespeare the only two documents surviving are the *entry of licence* and the *bond*. A note of the licence for the marriage of William Shakespeare and Anne Hathaway is recorded in the Bishop of Worcester's register for 27 November 1582. The licence granted only involved a single reading of the banns instead of the usual three. Such a document was necessary for a marriage at that time of the year, as three weeks' delay would have run into Advent, when weddings were not permitted. A subsequent failure to wed in January would have led to a clash with another prohibited season, meaning delay until April. The prospective bride would then have been eight months pregnant at the time of her marriage! The *entry of licence* is in the name of Bishop John Whitgift, later to become Archbishop of Canterbury. However, there is an anomaly with the licence as, though the bridegroom's name is spelt correctly, that of the bride is given as Anne Whateley of Temple Grafton (D8), rather than Hathaway of Shottery or Stratford. A number of theories have been given for the confusion over Anne's surname on this document. This second Anne appears nowhere else in any records. Did such a person ever exist? It was most probably a simple error made by an overworked ecclesiastical cleric who got his names mixed up. A number of errors with names occur in the register and, on the day the licence was applied for, the court had dealt with a case of non-payment of tithes involving a William Whateley of Crowle. The mystery of the 'Temple Grafton' bit might well be explained if the Hathaway family had any property or family links in the village. Another theory is that it is the name of a local girl with whom Will had been associating during his salad days. Whatever the reason, from the date of the bond and up to her death in 1623, Anne Hathaway was always identified as 'Mistress Shakespeare'. It is just another of the unsolved mysteries surrounding William Shakespeare.

Nonetheless, the marriage bond was signed by Will's two escorts, Sandells and Richardson, and posted on the following day, 28 November. It specified that 'William Shagspere and Anne hathwey of Stratford in the Diocese of Worcester maiden' could lawfully solemnise matrimony after one asking of the banns. Should the validity of the marriage be questioned then the sum of £40 of 'legal English money', posted by the two sureties, would be forfeited. The bond also indemnified the bishop against any impropriety in the issue of the license.

The register containing the entry of licence and the bond are both kept in a high security strong room at Worcester County Hall Record Office, the latter being set in a frame and secured to a wall. Both can be viewed by prior appointment (Tel: 01905 766351). The Record Office is adjacent to County Hall in Spetchley Road, Worcester – 2 miles (3.2km) from the city centre via A44 London Road, following signs to 'Countryside Centre' and 'County Hall'. It can also be reached from Junction 7 of the M5 motorway, following the same signage.

Worcester

Tel: 01905 726311 – Worcester TIC

Worcester is built on the banks of the River Severn and is vulnerable to flooding during winter months, with torrential downpours of rain and melting snow. At its heart is the magnificent cathedral, final resting place of King John (about whom Shakespeare was later to write one of his plays) and Prince Arthur, elder brother of King Henry VIII. The Prince was Katherine of Aragon's first husband and would have inherited the throne of England had he not died before his father, King Henry VII. The original fabric of the cathedral dates back to 1084, with a 14th century reconstruction, and is dedicated to Christ and the Blessed Virgin Mary. The nave is mostly 14th century work and part of the north choir transept dates from the 13th century, as do the choir and Lady Chapel. The Chapter House dates back to the early 12th century. Prince Arthur's Chantry, to the right of the high altar, is a richly decorated little chapel with some fine tracery. St Wulfstan's Crypt is the main survival of the earliest building and a superb example of Norman architecture.

It was from the top of the Cathedral's colossal central tower that Prince Charles Stuart watched the action at the Battle of Worcester in 1651, when Cromwell's forces defeated the Royalists and forced the prince to flee into hiding, whence, after many adventures, he escaped to France. He did not return to England until after Cromwell's death, when he was invited to accept the throne as Charles II. The Commandery in Worcester is a medieval timber-framed building open to the public and contains historic room settings and much information about the Civil War and the part the city played during that turbulent period in history.

On reaching College Yard, one can see across Lychgate to the statue of the composer Sir Edward Elgar, who had many close links with Worcester and whose work is frequently performed in the Three Choirs Festival which takes place every third year in the cathedral (in rotation with the nearby cathedrals of Hereford and Gloucester). Elgar's birthplace – now a museum dedicated to his memory – can be visited at the village of Lower Broadheath, three miles (5km) west of Worcester. His last resting place is in the churchyard at Little Malvern Priory, strikingly positioned on the slopes of the Malvern Hills.

There is much else to see in the city, including the lovely Georgian Guildhall, several historic churches, half-timbered buildings and museums, and the Royal Worcester Visitor Centre, where the world-famous pottery can be purchased direct from the manufacturer.

So what do we know of Anne Hathaway? A mile or so from home, young William Shakespeare courted his wife-to-be, who lived in the village of Shottery. 'Cottage' was something of a romantic 18th century misnomer used to describe the picturesque setting of her birthplace, a farmhouse known as Hewlands on the edge of the Forest of Arden. The Hathaways were yeomen farmers, comfortably off, working many hectares of land in the neighbourhood. Anne's grandfather, John

Hathaway, rented the property in 1546, and passed it on to his son, Richard, Anne's father. Her brother, Bartholomew, purchased the dwelling in 1610 and added a taller section to the western end of the house by the orchard (this part is now divided into three ground floor rooms, with two bedchambers above).The Hathaways occupied the house for several generations, until the male line ceased in 1746 with the death of John Hathaway. The property then passed, through John's sister Susanna, to his nephew, John Hathaway Taylor, whose son William lived there until his death in 1846. He was forced to sell the house six years before that due to financial difficulties, but remained as a tenant, as did his daughter, Mary, the wife of George Baker. She stayed there until 1892, when the property was taken over by the Shakespeare Birthplace Trust. They also inherited various items of furniture which had belonged to the family – including the Hathaway bed, which dated from the time of Anne. The building is a substantial timber-framed dwelling of twelve rooms, with a thatched roof, the whole setting often being described as 'the epitome of a typically English thatched cottage.'

Anne Hathaway's Cottage, Shottery (SH)

Tel: 01789 292100

The home of Shakespeare's wife before her marriage is one of England's most famous buildings. It is situated in Shottery, just over a mile (1.6km) west of Stratford. It was once a separate hamlet but now is linked to the town. The place has much Olde Worlde charm, with many lime-washed half-timbered buildings and quaint old cottages, some with thatched roofs and others with handmade tiling. Shottery can still be approached by using the footpaths of Shakespeare's day. At the far side of the village, almost hidden around a bend in the lane across Shottery Brook, is Anne Hathaway's Cottage.

Anne Hathaway's Cottage

The fabric of the house, which, apart from repairs following a fire in 1969, has suffered remarkably little restoration, belongs to several periods. When Shakespeare wooed his lady love at her family home he would have found a thatched cottage overlooking a farmyard. In the late 19th century, this area was transformed into a typical Victorian cottage garden. The visitor approaches the front of the Cottage along a path which wends its way through an array of penstemons, lupins, sweet peas, delphiniums, loosestrifes and clipped box hedges, which mingle with aromatic herbs such as fennel and feverfew. Red roses clamber up the wattle and daub walls of the building and others intertwine their branches along arches and pergolas. The oldest part of the building is to the right, dating from the mid-15th century. The part with the higher roofline, to the left, was probably added after 1623, and further alterations took place in 1697 with a rebuilding of the central chimneystack (bearing the initials 'JH' for John Hathaway).

The front door leads into a cross-passage and, turning left, one enters the hall, once used as the parlour. The hall has a large fireplace and on one side is a bacon cupboard, added in 1697. Also near the fireplace is an elm-boarded settle with a high back which was traditionally supposed to have been used by Anne and Will during their courting days. (Apart from the discomfort they would have experienced on such a hard piece of furniture, it is now known that it in fact dates from a later period.) There is a splendid late 17th century dresser with a display of 'Willow Pattern' plate crockery and pewter tableware. Leading off from the hall is a passageway of stone flags where a small room can be seen, which was once used as a buttery and for the brewing of ale. A second room was used as a cold store.

Moving to the upper level, the visitor climbs rather a creaking staircase, leading to a series of rooms used for sleeping and storage purposes. The first room contains items of furniture covering three centuries and includes a chair of woven straw, thought to be at least 350 years old. This room leads to the master bedchamber, which contains a magnificent ornately-carved bed, supposed to be the one valued at three pounds in Bartholomew Hathaway's will of 1624. The mattress on the bed is part-supported with threaded rope, which could be loosened or tightened according to the need. (This type of bed is thought to be the basis of the saying 'Good night, sleep tight'). There is another less elaborate bed from the same Tudor period in the adjoining room, which also has a doorway leading into a small storeroom. Here can be seen a section of open wall where plaster has been removed to expose the wattle and daub construction of the inside structure. The final first floor room was once used as a spare room for storage purposes.

Descending to ground floor level again we turn left into the original stone-flagged kitchen of Shakespeare's day. Parts of it have become shiny from the wear of millions of pairs of feet. The stone floor surface would have appeared rough in the 16th century and was possibly covered with rushes interspersed with herbs (remember this was once a farmhouse and all manner of unpleasant smells would have been trailed inside from muddy boots and shoes). Also in the kitchen is a large fireplace which would have acted as a communal area for the family and friends. To the left of the fireplace is a bread oven with a door made of elm wood for heat resistance, together with a long paddle used to move loaves in and out. Bellows are also on show as these would have been needed to maintain the correct temperature. Nearby is an early 16th century oak ark used for the storage of flour or bread.

Continuing on the tour, follow the cross-passage and exit to the rear of the house, before re-entering through a former parlour now used as an exhibition room. It contains items relating to the Hathaway family and other owners of the property, including a bonnet once worn by Mrs Mary Baker, who lived here in the 19th century and became the first guide for tourists. Stepping out into the front garden again, the visitor can perhaps spend a little time musing in the nearby orchard, or take the short walk to the Shakespeare Tree Garden, created in 1988, which includes many of the trees mentioned in Will's works. An Elizabethan-style yew maze has recently been introduced together with an exhibition of traditional and contemporary sculptures based on Shakespeare's plays – not all are to everyone's taste. Leaving the Cottage by the rear exit, some visitors may wish to cross over the road to see the quietly flowing Shottery Brook, a place said to have inspired the young poet in some of his works. For my part, the best time to see Anne Hathaway's Cottage and environs is either early morning before the coach loads of visitors descend upon the building, or later in the day when all is quiet again and a late afternoon sun peeps through the trees, casting a mellow glow over the whole landscape. These times are far more romantic and would undoubt-edly have inspired the young Will during his courtship days.

> *'Tis in ourselves that we are thus or thus*
> *Our bodies are our gardens to which our wills are gardeners*
>
> *Othello*, Act 1, Scene 3

Anne's father, Richard Hathaway – an acquaintance of John Shakespeare

– died in July 1582, prior to Anne's wedding to Will (possibly around the time his daughter conceived her first child). When he made his will in the preceding year, seven of Richard's children were living and he left legacies to each, including Anne (whom he addressed as Agnes). He bequeathed to her the sum of £6 13s 4d payable on the day of her marriage. Richard seems to have married twice and Anne, born in 1556, may well have been a child of the earlier marriage. His second wife, Joan, lived until 1599 and had at least five children through her marriage to Richard Hathaway.

There is still much speculation as to where the marriage of Anne and Will actually took place. This has never been determined. At many of the parishes where it could have occurred the relevant registers have not survived (as in the cases of Temple Grafton, Billesley and Luddington). Where registers do exist, no entry has been found – for example at St Michael's Parish Church, Worcester, which once stood right outside the Cathedral, but was demolished in the early 20th century. A register covering the period has survived but, unfortunately, the parchment pages bearing the marriage entries for 1582 have mysteriously been cut out, leaving just a tiny sliver of parchment attached to the sewings of the binding as witness to what has been removed. Were these pages extracted by an early souvenir hunter who had access to the documents? There is a strong local tradition that the marriage took place here.

There are two strong arguments for Temple Grafton as the place of Shakespeare's marriage. It has been suggested that Anne's mother came from there, and she could have been residing in the village since the death of Anne's father. Secondly the vicar, John Frith, was evaluated in a Puritan survey of the clergy in Warwickshire as 'an old priest and unsound in religion; he can neither preach nor read well, his chiefest trade is to cure hawks that are hurt or diseased, for which purpose many do usually repair to him.' Reading between the lines the old man may have been a 'soft touch', willing to perform ceremonies in the old Catholic tradition. Considering the desirability of a quick and quiet wedding, the location would undoubtedly have suited both families.

Temple Grafton

The present St Andrew's Church at Temple Grafton, built in grey and brown stone and featuring a tower with timber-framed bell-stage and spire, dates only from 1875. However, it replaced an earlier building of the Knights Templar, after which the village was named. Evidence

also points to a Saxon church belonging to Evesham Abbey being situated here in 710 AD.

Another possible location for Anne and Will's wedding is All Saints
Church, Billesley, which has a link with the Shakespeare family. It was
here, by tradition, that Shakespeare's last surviving descendant – his
granddaughter Elizabeth Nash (née Hall) – married her second husband,
John Barnard of Abingdon, in 1649. He was later knighted. Her first
husband was Thomas Nash, with whom she lived in the house next
door to New Place in Stratford. Elizabeth had no children from either
of her two marriages and she died in 1670. Unfortunately no parish
registers survive at All Saints from before 1816 to prove that either
Shakespeare or his granddaughter was married there.

Billesley

Billesley is a small hamlet to the west of Stratford, just off the A422
road to Alcester, and can be reached by lanes from Aston Cantlow and
Wilmcote. The immediate impression of All Saints Church is of a small
Georgian building of considerable rustic charm, with walls of the local
lias stone and mellow red-tiled roofs. It has been under the care of The
Churches Conservation Trust since 1976. At the time of writing, the
graveyard had become very overgrown with weeds and looked in
rather a sad state of neglect. However, the church is an architectural
gem and its interior has a warm feeling of compactness about it as you
enter. The origins of the building are found in the 11th century and it
stood in what was once an Anglo-Saxon settlement until the Black
Death in the mid-1330s wiped out the local population. The smallness
of the church gives credence to the idea that its isolation made it an
ideal place for a shotgun wedding, such as that of Anne and Will.

The fabric of the building provides evidence for a substantial
remodeling towards the middle of the 12th century, including a new
north aisle and portal with a fine tympanum. After the Black Death,
the north aisle was demolished. The fabric of the church had so deteriorated by the late 17th century that the new Lord of the Manor,
Bernard Whalley, is reputed to have rebuilt it in 1692. Many prominent
features in the present building were part of his work, such as the classical round-headed windows and the large south transept, later turned
into a vestry where the rector could have his food and refreshment
between services. The west gallery and box pews reflect the major
rebuilding, and the elegant fireplace and fine circular window in the

south transept mark where the occupants of the nearby hall had their pew. There are a number of memorials to prominent members of the manor and parish. (A key to the church is available from the Reception area of the nearby Billesley Manor, now an up-market hotel).

Billesley Manor is worthy of mention as, for generations, it belonged to the Trussells, one of whom was Speaker of the House of Commons when Edward II was denounced in 1327. Another member of the Trussell family was convicted of highway robbery and sentenced to death in 1588. The earlier manor house would undoubtedly have been familiar to William Shakespeare. As a youth, he may have poached deer on the estate. The present house was begun in 1610 by Sir Robert Lee, a Lord Mayor of London; it was later the home of Thomas Sherlock, successively Bishop of Bangor, Salisbury and London. In 1980 the building was converted into a hotel. Nearby, on the site of the old Saxon village, a rectangular 17th century dovecote still remains. Billesley is a place where time has stood still, apart from in the modern amenities of the hotel.

Luddington

Luddington sits on the banks of the River Avon 2 miles (3.2km) west of Stratford. It is a charming, typical Warwickshire village, comprising a few black-and-white cottages and some later housing built after the 1930s. Still another tradition exists that William Shakespeare married Anne Hathaway in the old chapel, which was burnt down towards the end of the 18th century. All records in the old church were destroyed with the exception of the Bishops' Bible (1568) and the old stone font, both of which have been carefully preserved. A new church was built and consecrated in 1872, sited on land donated by the Marquis of Hertford, a major landowner. Yet again, there is no positive proof that Will's marriage actually took place here. It is another tradition which has passed down the generations of local residents.

Once the wedding was over, not being able to afford a home of their own, the young couple would no doubt have gone back to live at the family house in Henley Street, Stratford, to await the arrival of their firstborn infant. After Will's independence following school, married life may quickly have proved a millstone around his neck. Most probably he became bored with the domestic routine of home life, got itchy feet, and discovered a deep yearning to follow in the footsteps of the groups of travelling players and entertainers who passed through Stratford. Like most young men who find themselves tied down to an early marriage, he would have needed some outlets for his natural exuberance. This began for him a period of restlessness which would soon change his life.

Heaven is above all yet; there sits a Judge
that no king can corrupt

Henry VIII, Act 3, Scene 1

CHAPTER 5

Family Responsibilities

ANNE AND WILL'S first child, a daughter, was born six months after their marriage and baptised by the Reverend Henry Heicroft at Holy Trinity Church, Stratford, on Trinity Sunday, 26 May 1583. The baby was named Susanna Shakespeare, a name with Old Testament origins and usually attributed to Puritan leanings.

From the day of his marriage, William Shakespeare's life began to change. The couple is thought to have set up home with Will's parents in Henley Street, which would already have been overcrowded with his younger brothers and sole surviving sister Joan. It would have been a far from ideal arrangement and must have caused a few family problems and frustrations for Anne and Will. The early days of the marriage are still something of a mystery – part of the 'lost' years. The strongest assumption is that he was working with his father in the wool and leather gloving business run from their home address. It has, however, also been suggested that Will worked for a time for a solicitor or in some legal capacity as later, in some of his writings, he appears to possess an in-depth knowledge of the legal system. Others have mentioned that he worked as a trainee lawyer, butcher, doctor, gardener or 'as a schoolmaster in the country'.

Anne, after the arrival of their first child, would have become fully immersed in motherhood and domestic chores. Their lack of privacy and growing family must have been a source of tension and perhaps led to a rift in both their domestic and marital relationships, giving Will a yearning for some form of escapism. There were other problems looming on the horizon with regard to religious matters.

Despite the purge on Roman Catholics by Elizabeth's court during the Edmund Campion and Jesuit priests episode, plots were being discovered with the similar aim of deposing the English Queen in favour of Mary Queen of Scots. Matters started to come to a head within months of Anne and Will's marriage and involved some leading Catholic families from across Warwickshire.

In October 1583, a man named John Somerville, from Edstone near Stratford, was arrested beside an inn at Aynho (B18), on the road to London. He was caught making allegations about Queen Elizabeth, proclaiming he was going up to London to assassinate her. Somerville had been educated at New College, Oxford, where he became a Fellow. After settling in Warwickshire he married Margaret Arden, daughter of Edward Arden, head of the Arden family. Somerville appears to have been mentally deranged, but his wife was described by the prosecution as 'a very perverse and malicious Papist' whose faith had been strengthened by a visit to the Continent.

The Saxon Sanctuary, Wootton Wawen
Tel: 01564 792659

Edstone Hall was once the stronghold of the Somervilles (since when it has been rebuilt). It was part of the manor of Wootton priory, of which the Cistercian monks of Bordesley Abbey near Redditch had been granted much of the estate. The manor was passed down from the Aylesbury family to the Somervilles in the 1400s. One of the most famous of the family was a poet, William Somerville, who wrote one of his more famous works, *The Chase*, while living there. His tomb and monument can be seen in the splendid Saxon Sanctuary of St Peter's at Wootton Wawen (D13), thought to be the oldest Saxon church in Warwickshire and situated 8 miles (13km) from Stratford. The building is notable for its contents, which include a beautiful 15th century carved oak screen and pulpit, two old chests ornamented with wrought iron, and several fine monuments and brasses. The church is open to the public and there is a colourful and explicit *Forest of Arden* exhibition in the barn-roofed Lady Chapel. It traces the history of the woodland village and surrounding area.

Edward Arden's Catholicism was well known and, earlier, he had been suspected of aiding and abetting the Jesuit priests in their mission. When John Somerville's rantings were made public at the English court, they sparked off another witch-hunt of prominent Catholic families who might have supported such a scheme. The most powerful Warwickshire Puritan at Elizabeth's court was Robert Dudley, Earl of Leicester, who in 1575 had entertained Queen Elizabeth at Kenilworth Castle. It was he who undertook to root out the instigators, with assistance from Sir Thomas Lucy of Charlecote. A warrant was drawn up for the arrest of anyone found to be co-operating with known Catholic conspirators. Lord Leicester and Edward Arden had been enemies for some years and the former would have seized the opportunity to investigate his rival. Systematic searches took place of known Catholic houses in the Midlands, hunting for suspects and evidence of conspiracies. The Ardens were targetted and the family seat of Park Hall – which once stood near to Coleshill but is now almost obliterated by urban development – was ransacked. The web of intrigue was easy to trace as there had been much inter-marriage between local Catholic families. A particularly strong tie was between Edward Arden and the powerful Throckmorton family of Coughton Court near Alcester. Edward had once been a ward of the family and had married their daughter, Mary.

Coughton Court, nr Alcester (NT)
Tel: 01789 400777

Coughton Court is two miles (3km) north of Alcester in the Vale of Arrow on the A435. The Throckmorton family have lived there since 1409, when they acquired it by marriage with the de Cocton family. The house is mainly Elizabethan, but the structure, like its furnishings and decorations, is a blend of several periods. The stone gatehouse was built by Sir George Throckmorton around 1518 and was later incorporated into the west front. It is flanked by stucco wings with 18th century ogee-headed windows and has a fan-vaulted gateway – now the entrance hall – which leads to a three-sided court, with timber-framed north and south wings and a knot garden layout.

The family was very prominent in Tudor times and instigated much Catholic emancipation. Coughton Court was a stronghold of resistance and one of the haunts frequented by the conspirators responsible for the Gunpowder Plot in 1605. Some of the additions and alterations have been the result of military operations – Coughton Court was occupied by Parliamentarians, bombarded by Royalist forces in 1643–44 during the Civil War, and pillaged by an anti-Catholic mob in 1688 during the reign of James II. The building also contains two priest holes, both in the same gatehouse turret. The family used a chapel within the house until relaxation of laws against Catholics allowed them to build their own church in 1857. The site therefore has the distinction of having two churches – the other being a parish church dating from the late 15th century which has much original glass and woodwork. The contents of the house include notable furniture and porcelain together with many portraits, Jacobite relics and items relating to the family's history. Of particular interest is the chemise thought to have been worn by Mary Queen of Scots at her execution at Fotheringhay Castle

(E21) on 8 February 1587. Sir Nicholas Throckmorton had been one of the English ambassadors during Queen Mary's reign in Scotland.

In November 1583, Elizabeth's 'Spy Catcher', Sir Francis Walsingham, received information that Francis Throckmorton, a Catholic cousin of Sir Nicholas, had been carrying letters to and from Mary Queen of Scots. The Earl of Northumberland was also implicated in the Throckmorton plot and sent to the Tower. Details of the scheme included the invasion of England by the Spanish and the release of the Scottish Queen. Francis Throckmorton was duly arrested and taken to the Tower (A7). Edward Arden, John Somerville and other members of their families, along with Arden's priest, Father Hall, were also arrested. Each man was subjected to interrogation by torture on the rack whilst the women were verbally examined and kept in solitary confinement.

The trials were held at the Guildhall in London and John Somerville, Edward Arden, his wife, and Father Hall were each charged with conspiracy against the Crown and sentenced to death. Fortunately, Mistress Arden's life was spared. Somerville was found dead in Newgate prison the morning after receiving his sentence – either he took his own life or he was murdered by persons unknown. Edward Arden was dragged to a place of execution at Smithfield (A5), hung, castrated, disemboweled and had his innards burnt in front of his eyes. His body was then butchered and cut into sections – the head being displayed on London Bridge and other parts being sent off for show at prominent sites as a warning to others.

After the arrest of Edward Arden, Sir Thomas Lucy's investigations into Catholic families became more intense. The fact that the Shakespeares of Stratford were kinsmen of the Ardens would undoubtedly have put them under scrutiny. They may have been thoroughly investigated and had a warrant issued for a search of their premises. Perhaps that was the reason why, for fear of discovery, John Shakespeare hid his own Catholic 'testament of faith' in the eaves of his Henley Street home?

The purge of Catholic houses in Warwickshire continued through December 1583 and January 1584, routing out anyone who had either assisted Jesuit priests or been involved in conspiracies against the Crown. There is no doubt that Lucy built up considerable hostility from the Papists by his constant pursuit, torment and examination of their motives and movements. Will Shakespeare was still only nineteen, married with one child, when he was likely subjected to a house search at the home he and Anne shared with his parents and family.

In May 1584 Anne conceived again, and twins were born nine

months later. They were baptised at Holy Trinity Church on 2 February 1585. They were a boy and a girl and named Hamnet and Judith after two close friends, the Sadlers, who lived in Stratford at the corner of High Street and Sheep Street. It is thought these friends were also godparents to the two infants. Hamnet Sadler was to become a lifelong friend of Will. It is around this time that one of the early myths of Will's life is based.

The evil that men do lives after them;
the good is often interred with their bones

Julius Caesar, Act 3, Scene 2

Due to frustrations with his early marriage, Shakespeare was, according to tradition, always a little wild, rather fond of drinking, and subject, at times, to outrageous behaviour. The story goes that he was discovered and arrested for poaching deer in Charlecote Park, the home of Sir Thomas Lucy. Will was brought before the magisterial owner, who ordered the lad be whipped. In retaliation, Shakespeare composed some abusive verse about Lucy which he displayed upon the gatehouse at Charlecote, which redoubled the prosecution and led to the poacher's eventual flight from Stratford to London. So began his career. Later, in retaliation, Shakespeare caricatured Sir Thomas in *Henry IV, Part II*, and *The Merry Wives of Windsor*, as the fussy, self-opinionated Justice Shallow. The arms of the Lucy family include a rebus consisting of three luces – an ancient name for a freshwater pike. In *The Merry Wives of Windsor*, Will gives Justice Shallow a coat of arms including a 'dozen white luces'.

The 'poaching' story originated in the 17th century but has, over recent years, been hotly disputed. For a start, the Lucy family did not keep manorial deer in the 16th century though there was much poaching across the county during the 1580s due to poverty and shortage of food. There were, however, many wild deer which roamed around the countryside of the Forest of Arden – some of which may have strayed onto the Charlecote estate. Even the Shakespeare family may for a period have had a job to make ends meet, especially considering the crumbling state of John's glove-making and wool business in Stratford. Whatever the truth, Sir Thomas would most probably already have been an enemy of the family after his earlier investigations. He may well have made an example of the lad and inflicted undue punishment upon him.

Charlecote Park (NT)

An avenue of limes leads to Charlecote Park, a massive Elizabethan mansion set in fine, open parkland where deer now roam. The beautiful, rosy pink-bricked Elizabethan gatehouse is an architectural gem from the Tudor period and is in its original state. It has two octagonal towers facing the park, with ogee-shaped cupolas, and under the arch is heavy stone vaulting. The clock in the south turret is dated 1824. Sir Thomas Lucy I, who instigated the Catholic witch-hunts, pulled down the original family house and built this red-brick mansion on the site between 1551–58. It was the first great Elizabethan house to be erected in Warwickshire. Its early history dates from 1189, when the estate was given by Henry de Montfort to Thurstan de Charlecote, whose grandson assumed the name of Lucy. The house continued without a break in the Lucy family until 1945, when it was presented to the National Trust. The private family wing is still occupied by the present baronet, Sir Edmund Fairfax-Lucy, and his family.

It was at Charlecote that Robert Dudley, Earl of Leicester, deputising for his Queen, knighted Thomas Lucy in 1565. Queen Elizabeth spent two nights there in 1572 on her way to Kenilworth Castle as Leicester's guest. The mansion stands on a terrace above the River Avon, overlooking the flat meadows where Charles I is thought to have camped with his army in 1642 on the night prior to the Battle of Edge Hill. Although some of Sir Thomas Lucy's Great Hall survives, the house was largely remodeled in the 19th century, with heavy carved fireplaces, elaborate plasterwork and decorations.

After passing through the gatehouse, the house is approached by crossing the forecourt and heading into the front entrance, which is of Renaissance design and emblazoned with the arms of Queen Elizabeth. Turning left, the visitor moves into the morning room, still in use by the family, and on to the Great Hall. Over the fireplace are busts of Sir Thomas Lucys I and II, and one of Queen Elizabeth. This was copied from Maximilian Colt's tomb effigy in Westminster Abbey (A14), with the addition of a crown. Left of the dining room door is a bust of William Shakespeare. There is also a bust of the first Sir Thomas's wife, Lady Joyce Lucy, which looks remarkably like similar effigies of Mary Queen of Scots.

Nearly every generation of the Lucy family since the first Sir Thomas is included in the various portraits which hang in this chamber. It is just one of a series of sumptuous rooms in the house tour which are full of family portraits, heraldic stained glass, sculptures, and other priceless furniture and effects. In the nearby service wing, one can see a scullery, kitchen, laundry and brew house. Other outbuildings include a coach house, stable carriage houses and a tack room. The grounds and park were laid out in 1760 by the famous landscape gardener, Capability Brown, and are little changed. A recent addition is a sensory garden for the partially impaired which was officially opened in July 2002, by actress Dame Judi Dench.

Family tombs can be seen in St Leonard's Church in the nearby village of Charlecote. They have survived from the original 12th century church, which was demolished to make way for the present building of high Gothic design, consecrated four years after the demolition in 1853. It has a distinctive and elegant spire and the interior is richly adorned and fitted with oak. There is a Lucy family vault with three original alabaster tombs – those of the first Sir Thomas Lucy, his son and grandson (both also named Sir Thomas) – featuring effigies in reclining positions.

Charlecote Park is open to the public during the tourist season and it is good to see how and where a Warwickshire aristocratic family such as the Lucys lived during the days of William Shakespeare. Whether or not there is any grain of truth in the poaching story, it certainly adds a touch of romanticism to the visit.

But words are words: I never yet did hear
That the bruised heart was pierced through the ear

Othello, Act 1, Scene 3

The frustrations of an early marriage and fatherhood must have rankled with Will and he no doubt yearned for the carefree life enjoyed by single men. Yet he had a wife and family to feed and clothe and he could only do so by working in some trade or profession. The situation was not helped by John Shakespeare's fall from grace as he got into greater debt and was removed from the august Town Council. This wouldn't have reflected well on Will, who perhaps felt it was time to make his own way in the world. It is most likely that Shakespeare had already been smitten by the acting bug when he watched various groups of players as they performed in Stratford's Guildhall and other surrounding places such as Kenilworth and Coventry. Whatever work he undertook locally, he did not stay in the town of his birth for very long. The time of his actual departure is still open to speculation.

One story is that he was tempted to London through news of his fellow Stratfordian, Richard Field, and all he was achieving in the metropolis. Field had become apprenticed to a London printer, Thomas Vautrollier, and later married his master's widow. Richard and Will were soon to become associated as publisher and author. It has also been said that Will joined a troupe of travelling actors, as a number of these passed through Stratford about this time. They included the Earl of Worcester's Men in 1582, the Earl of Essex's Men in 1584 and the Queen's Men in 1587. Perhaps he went to London with one of these. The Earl of Worcester's leading player was Edward Alleyn, two years younger than Will. The most successful company of that decade, the Queen's Men, were headed by the leading clown of the day, Richard Tarlton. The majority of actors in the Queen's Men had previously worked with James Burbage in the Earl of Leicester's Men, some already having made names for themselves. These players had been specially chosen for Queen Elizabeth and arrived in Stratford in 1587 when Shakespeare was just twenty-three. Corporation accounts reveal they gave the Queen's Men the largest sum ever paid out for any visiting troupe – a total of twenty shillings, plus another sixteen pence to cover costs of repair of a bench which had been damaged during a performance. Prior to reaching Stratford, the troupe had performed in Abingdon and Thame in the Thames Valley and, whilst in Thame (B16), an incident occurred in White Hound Close when two actors – William Knell and John Towne of Shoreditch – became involved in a drunken brawl. The result was that Towne badly wounded his partner, Knell, who died within the space of half an hour. This meant the troupe was short of players.

It so happened that within two days of the killing, the Queen's Men were in Stratford. Perhaps they found in Will a volunteer who was ready and prepared to travel with them to replace the lately deceased actor. The outcome of the incident was that Towne, after pleading self-defence, was pardoned by the Thame coroner and, later, by the Queen. Within twelve months, the late William Knell's wife married another actor, John Heminges, who was to become a close companion of Shakespeare and, indeed, one of the two collaborators who put together the *First Folio* of his collected plays. He also became a beneficiary of his will.

One can only imagine the scene between Shakespeare and his wife and parents, after he announced his imminent departure from Stratford. There may have been some degree of sympathy but more likely a fear of insecurity gripped Anne as she contemplated the lonely life which lay ahead of her. On the other hand, perhaps the marriage had turned sour and both needed some space. Whatever the reason, it would seem that Will was determined on his own course of action – though he was to keep in touch with his family and visit Stratford as and when circumstances allowed. Opportunity was knocking at Will's door and he grasped it with both hands. He was on the edge of an exciting new world and career – the most important turning point in his life!

> *This fellow is wise enough to play the fool,*
> *and to do that well craves a kind of wit*
>
> *Twelfth Night*, Act 3, Scene 1

CHAPTER 6

London and the Theatre

WILLIAM SHAKESPEARE MUST have felt both excited and apprehensive as he left his Stratford birthplace. It is not known whether he went direct to London or if he travelled with one of the touring companies on their scheduled visits to various towns and cities around the country. There is no documentary evidence of such. He may well have done so and reached London as part of one of their itineraries, perhaps parting company with them to make his own way in the metropolis. Whyever he left them, he would have found the acting experience gained was invaluable when coming to terms with his new trade as a professional actor. His fellow players would undoubtedly have made a great impression upon the young man and he was later to put his touring experiences to good use by copying plots from some of their productions in at least half a dozen of his own plays. If he made his own way to London from Stratford, he would have either walked or ridden – perhaps by a post-horse or a horse of his own – depending on finances. On a good surface and at a reasonably good pace on horseback, ten miles (16km) could be covered in an hour. Leaving Stratford, Will would have crossed over the Clopton Bridge and made his way south.

There were two routes he could have taken. The first was the road through Banbury, Bicester, Aylesbury and Amersham; the second via Chipping Norton, Oxford and High Wycombe. Both roads met at Uxbridge for the western route into London. By most accounts, Shakespeare preferred the way through Oxford, and the Crown Tavern, situated in an courtyard just off the east side of Cornmarket Street, was long said to be one of his resting places. Whichever route he chose, Will would have found that wayside inns were numerous, hospitable, and well appointed.

His first impressions of London are not recorded but, after having lived in a comparatively small and mainly agricultural Warwickshire town, he would have been amazed by the enormity of the city, its smells, the poverty, and the many thousands of people, horses and other domestic animals. Buildings ranged from low taverns, tenements and poor housing to elegant mansions, large palaces and places of government.

The largest structure was the original Gothic-style St Paul's Cathedral (burnt down in 1666 and replaced by the existing masterpiece built by Sir Christopher Wren). It must all have been quite overpowering for the young Shakespeare, and no doubt came as a distinct contrast with Stratford. Even London's main river, the tidal Thames, bore no comparison to the gently-flowing Avon which Will had left behind.

Roman London (*Londinium*) had been built on the north bank. The city wall which encircled it was bow-shaped, curving north west from the Tower of London and then turning westwards and south; an arc of over two miles (3.2km), down to a point on the river near the present Blackfriars Bridge. The wall then followed the riverside back to where it started. The landward side was still intact in Elizabethan times, but the section of wall by the river had, by then, disappeared. At the eastern end stood the mighty fortress, the Tower of London, place of fortification, state prison and regular site for executions. Gates into the city had been erected at Tower Postern, Aldgate, Bishopsgate, Moorgate, Cripplegate, Aldersgate, Newgate and Ludgate. Main routes into the city were the Old Kent Road – for travellers to and from the south and the Continent – the Great North Road – from the north and Scotland – and the one used by Shakespeare – from western destinations and Wales.

The institution of the Inns of Court at the western end had encouraged expansion of the city along Holborn and Fleet Street, Temple Bar marking its new western fringe. The mansions of distinguished noblemen tended to cluster to the south of the Strand, not far from the edge of the river. In Shakespeare's day, the only crossing of the Thames was the original London Bridge, which connected the City with the south bank in Surrey, close to the former St Mary Overie church, now Southwark Cathedral (A17). This area was known as Bankside – the home of seafarers, beggars, ruffians, drunkards, thieves and other rougher elements of society – and possessed a range of dwellings which included prisons, theatres, taverns, countless brothels, cock pits, bear-baiting pits, bowling alleys, gaming houses and poor housing. Most of the land and property in Bankside belonged to the Bishop of Winchester, whose responsibility it was to try and curtail the activities of the brothels, though he still derived rents from them. He also maintained a prison on his land, known as the Clink, a name which has remained synonymous with jails to this day. With it on Clink Street are the remains of the Bishop's Palace, which would have been familiar to Will.

London had become a thriving port and on both sides of the river wharves and warehouses had been established to service overseas trade and sea-going craft, as had several Thames-side towns further upstream (Windsor Castle (B12) and the Royal Palaces of Whitehall (A13), Hampton Court (B11) and Richmond (B10) are all in that direction). The waterside was not a pretty sight and was overrun with vermin which fed off garbage and sewage floating in the river. It was an obnoxious breeding ground for plague and disease.

A pattern of separate communities had sprung up beyond the city walls – places such as Kensington, Islington, Hackney and Bow. Further away lay other villages at Hammersmith, Hampstead, Hornsey, Highgate, Tottenham and Barking. Westminster, though quite close, was in fact a separate city reached from Charing Cross, then a rural settlement, by a route which once led in the direction of the present Parliament Street.

By the time of Shakespeare's arrival, the population of London must have been about 200,000 and steadily growing, as more people flocked to the big city in search of work and perhaps fame or fortune. The major livery companies were well established, gaining influence and power in City life. A decisive event had just taken place in religious politics with the execution of Mary Queen of Scots in 1587. Queen Mary had become the figurehead of the Roman Catholic movement to regain the English throne from the Protestant Queen Elizabeth. The Scottish Queen's death was something of a watershed for the scaling down of the persecution of English Catholic families.

However, other Continental pressure resulted in the sailing of the Spanish Armada in the following year – it was comprehensively defeated by Sir Francis Drake off Plymouth Sound. This action caused the upsurge of much patriotism towards Elizabeth throughout England. It helped suppress the Catholic cause, though pockets of resistance still festered in places like Warwickshire among such aristocratic families as the Throckmortons, Catesbys, and others. Those still faithful to their religion continued to celebrate the Mass in clandestine places.

So what did Shakespeare do when he first arrived in London? Where did he stay? And how soon did he start to act or become a playwright? Unfortunately, his arrival was still part of the 'lost' years and one can only surmise through reported hearsay or later documentation as to what the answers might be.

There is a tradition that he started out as a horse-holder; this was first mentioned by Sir William Davenant, a poet and theatre manager who claimed he met Shakespeare when he stayed at his father's Oxford inn, the Crown Tavern, on his way to London. He also claimed to be Will's godson. It is possible that Shakespeare attended Davenant's baptism in nearby St Martin's Church, whose tower is over 600 years old. Davenant told Thomas Betterton (a leading actor of the Restoration) that when Will first arrived in London 'he was without money and friends, and, being a stranger, knew not to whom to apply nor by what means to support himself.' However, Shakespeare already knew Richard Field, the printer, from their boyhood days in Stratford – their fathers were close associates in the tannery industry – and there was also William Combe, who became a barrister at Middle Temple. It is therefore quite likely he made his way to meet either one or both of these former colleagues.

Shakespeare not only had to earn a living but also to gain the necessary theatrical experience to master his craft. The obvious course was to join up with one of the companies of actors. Generally there were about eight men in each troupe, who often invested their own savings in a number of plays and costumes. Profits accrued from their efforts were divided according to the percentage that each had invested. There were usually three or four boys, apprentice actors, who were trained to play female roles, along with a few casual novices hired for the occasion. Will probably got his first foothold in the theatre as one of these 'hirelings', both helping backstage and taking on the occasional acting role. He was first given an opportunity to tread the boards in London at about the same time as a poet named Robert Greene started to write manuscripts.

Through tatter'd clothes small vices appear;
Robed and furr'd gowns hide all

King Lear, Act 4, Scene 6

The Earl of Leicester's Men were the first organised acting company, formed in 1572 from the earl's own household when Will was about eight years old. They performed at court the following year and the company was granted a licence by royal patent. On the death of their patron in 1588, the Earl of Leicester's Men were merged with Ferdinando, Lord Strange's Men (he later became the Earl of Derby and had connections with Sir Thomas Hesketh in Lancashire. As stated earlier, some believe it was Sir Thomas who first found employment for the young Will Shakespeare as an actor/schoolmaster at one or other of Derby's residences). This company toured the country and for the next six years they were also associated with the Admiral's Men. Together, they performed at both The Theatre and the Rose, where they are thought to have staged some of Shakespeare's earlier plays. The Earl of Derby died in 1590, and his place as patron was successively filled by Henry Carey, 1st Lord Hunsdon, who died in July 1596, and his son and heir, George Carey, 2nd Lord Hunsdon. This gentleman became Lord Chamberlain in March 1597 and, for the time being, the group of players became known as the Lord Chamberlain's Men. They included William Shakespeare and it is thought he spent much of his acting career with them.

In 1576, when Will was twelve, work began on the building of the first public playhouse in London at a site in Shoreditch (A2), then a growing suburb to the north of the City wall. The scheme was the brainchild of James Burbage, a former actor with the Earl of Leicester's Men. He obtained a 21-year lease and permission to build The Theatre, named after Roman amphitheatres, about a mile (1.6km) outside the Bishopsgate entrance to the City. There is a commemorative plaque on 86-88 Curtain Road. (The word 'theatre' was not in regular usage at the time.) Burbage lived with his two sons, Richard and Cuthbert, in nearby Holywell Lane. Shakespeare acted at The Theatre and may have lodged somewhere south of Shoreditch High Street. (Richard Burbage, fellow actor William Sly, and former Tudor court jester William Tarlton, are each buried at the local parish church of St Leonard's (A1) at the top of Shoreditch High Street. The churchyard is now a garden.)

There were good reasons for Shoreditch being chosen as the site for a theatre; chiefly it was beyond the city wall and would not come under the jurisdiction of the civic authorities, yet was close enough to enjoy the patronage of city audiences and many prominent people. Compared with holding performances within the confines of an inn yard (where the sale of ale and other commodities was the most important factor) a custom-built playhouse provided better facilities for audiences, allowing greater concentration for actors. Once permission was granted, James Burbage moved quickly with his plans and the building was duly constructed as a wooden amphitheatre of two or three galleries, surrounding an open arena with a form of apron stage, to allow maximum viewing of the actors by the audience.

The Theatre was of a circular or polygonal structure, about thirty feet high and fifty feet across. Three storeys of seating galleries projected into the circle from the outer walls to a depth of twelve feet. The perimeter seating was roofed with thatch, leaving the central area open to the elements. Over the stage was a large canopy supported by heavy pillars. During winter months and inclement weather, actors continued their work at inn yards in order to save their patrons having to trudge through the ice, snow and occasional storm.

In order to plough back any profits into the scheme, Burbage opened The Theatre in 1576, prior to its completion in 1577. In that year, a rival theatre named the Curtain was opened by Henry Laneman at nearby Finsbury. The new theatre was situated in a dingy alley called Curtain Close (now Hewett Street); the site is now marked by a plaque on rather a mundane building.

Cowards die many times before their deaths:
the valiant never taste of death but once

Julius Caesar, Act 2, Scene 2

Ever since the days of Henry VIII, the court had appointed a Master of the Revels, a sort of court jester, whose responsibility it was to arrange entertainment over the Christmas season. It was also his job to grant a licence for plays to be performed in public. The bearer of the title between 1579–1607 was Edmund Tilney, a man who was to become an important figure in the realm of English literature, by selecting and staging Shakespeare's works for some of the most influential people of the time. He worked from an office at Clerkenwell in the converted priory of St John, of which only the Gatehouse remains (A3); it is situated in St John's Lane.

In 1583, Queen Elizabeth requested that Tilney choose 'a company of players for her Majesty' and the Queen's Men were established at Burbage's Theatre, proving unrivalled in the theatre scene for over five years. They appeared at court on a regular basis and played in Stratford in 1587. At some point around this time, Shakespeare, a member of the Earl of Leicester's Men, became affiliated to the Queen's Men and would often take to the stage with them. As well as performing in London, they toured the country, playing in various towns.

Richard Tarlton was the leading performer of the newly-formed Queen's Men and popular in court circles. (He was born in 1530 at the village of Condover (E16), four miles (3.2km) south of Shrewsbury. He is thought to have lived in a cottage in the area of Pyepits, on the site of the present Condover Hall, a fine Elizabethan mansion completed in 1598.) He was to become a highly successful actor and court jester to the Queen, and played the fool both onstage and in the audience.

His popularity was so great that many hostelries and taverns chose to use his image on their signs. Tarlton was also a writer, with a play to his credit based on the seven deadly sins. He died in September 1588, was much mourned, and, as mentioned earlier, was buried at St Lawrence's Church, Shoreditch. Tarlton is thought to have been the original of 'poor Yorick' in Shakespeare's *Hamlet*; the 'fellow of infinite jest, of most excellent fancy', whose skull features in the graveyard scene.

A third theatre, the Rose, was erected in the area of Bankside shortly after the formation of the Queen's Men. It was financed by Philip Henslowe, a pawnbroker and moneylender who in 1585 took out a lease on a prominently-sited piece of land. The Rose became the base for Lord Strange's Men. (In 1989, the foundations of the Rose Theatre were discovered and excavated under what is now the Rose Court building. The site in Park Street, around the corner from Shakespeare's Globe (A16), is open to visitors, who can see the exposed foundations of the Rose Theatre and an exhibition about its history.)

It could have been at the Rose Theatre that Shakespeare first saw Edward Alleyn, one of the greatest actors of the period. Alleyn was one of the original members of the Earl of Worcester's Men and had become the leading actor of the Admiral's Men. Their patron was Charles Howard, 2nd Baron Howard of Effingham, the Lord High Admiral of the Fleet, who diverted the Spanish Armada. Edward Alleyn was to play the leading role in Christopher Marlowe's masterpiece, *Tamburlaine the Great*, and both his performance and the play were received to great acclaim. When Richard Tarlton died, the Queen's Men lost their foremost performer. Eyes began to turn on Alleyn, who soon became a rich man. In 1592, he married Joan Woodward, the step-daughter of Philip Henslowe, and Alleyn's fortunes became tied to Henslowe and the Rose Theatre. (He became more involved with Bankside when he was made Master of the Royal Bears, Bulls and Mastiff Dogs in 1604, the year in which he bought the Manor of Dulwich. A man of many talents, Alleyn was a musician and public benefactor. In 1619 he founded the College of God's Gift, the forerunner of Dulwich College – portraits of Alleyn, Woodward and Henslowe hang in Dulwich Picture Gallery).

With the advent of new venues and new troupes came a demand for new drama and new writers. There was soon no shortage of young men to feed the theatre with plays and ideas; in the main, they had been educated at either Oxford or Cambridge universities. This group of poets and playwrights introduced a new fashion for blank verse, romance, bawdy comedy, tragedy and grandiose dialogue. Between them, they were to provide the young Will with a list of ideas and plots which he would later incorporate into much of his own writing. As well as Robert Greene and Christopher Marlowe, Shakespeare's contemporaries included Thomas Lodge, George Peele, Thomas Nashe and John Lyly.

The actor, poet and playwright Robert Greene made a considerable impact – he was an intellectual, had received a University education, and specialised in writing on the subject of love without making it sound too frivolous. This was rather odd as he earlier lived the life of a wanton and travelled on the continent for several years before gravitating towards London and theatre life. It is thought he rather scorned Shakespeare's lack of a University background and probably there was an element of jealousy in Greene. In 1592 he attacked Shakespeare in a pamphlet entitled *Greene's Groatsworth of Witte*, describing him as 'an upstart crow, beautified with our feathers'. This would suggest that, during his time with the Earl of Leicester's Men, Will was beginning to make quite a name for himself.

But Christopher Marlowe is probably the most important and certainly the best-remembered of the bright young playwrights. He was a close friend of Greene. Marlowe was born in Canterbury (B8) in 1564, the son of a shoemaker, and was educated at the local grammar school until he matriculated at Corpus Christi College in Cambridge. Three years later he obtained his BA, and in 1587 started to study for his MA. He eventually arrived in London as a keen, thrusting and ambitious graduate with a fresh mind and ideas all his own, and was reputed to be both an atheist and a homosexual. The contacts he gained at Cambridge undoubtedly helped in London, and he soon started to write plays. *Tamburlaine the Great* (in two parts) was first presented in 1587, and was considered the best tragedy yet produced for the English stage. *Doctor Faustus, The Jew of Malta* and *Edward II* followed over the next three years. Marlowe was employed by Lord Strange (the Earl of Derby), then by the Lord Chamberlain following Strange's death in 1594.

At some time, Marlowe was also employed by Sir Francis Walsingham, Elizabeth's 'Spy Catcher'. On 2 October 1587 Christopher Marlowe is mentioned as a courier in despatches from Utrecht in Holland to the Secretary of State.

He was arrested in September 1589 for taking part in a duel in Finsbury. He and another poet, Thomas Watson, were accused of murdering an innkeeper's son and taken to Newgate Prison, but were acquitted on 3 December. He lived to see another day and write another play! Unfortunately, Marlowe did not see that many more days as he was involved in a pub brawl in rather mysterious circumstances on 30 May 1593 and was subsequently murdered. Marlowe's death was a great loss to the English stage. However, some of his supporters claimed his death had been a sham, that he had escaped to Italy and, afterwards, forwarded his manuscripts to a literary agent called 'William Shakespeare'. A rather unlikely story!

Some modern commentators claim that Shakespeare's plays were really written by Christopher Marlowe. Others have indicated Francis Bacon, a statesman and great contemporary prose writer, philosopher and lawyer. It is argued that Shakespeare's plays embody a far greater knowledge and understanding, especially of law, than he could ever have possessed. Among his contemporaries only Bacon had such knowledge and understanding. It is also thought there are many parallelisms between passages in Shakespeare's and Bacon's works, such as references to the Bible and ancient classics. Another claimant for the authorship of the plays is Edward de Vere, 17th Earl of Oxford. He was of noble birth and came from an academic background, had the necessary experience, and used the nom de plume 'William Shakespeare.' The fact that he died in 1604 and ten of Will's plays were not written until after that date rather rules him out of the running.

The fact is that nobody with any in-depth knowledge of the Shakespearean era has proven that the plays were written by any other than Shakespeare himself. It has never been explained why some of the people closest to Will – John Heminges, Henry Condell, Robert Greene, Henry Chettle and Ben Jonson – all left documentation to their awareness that William Shakespeare, the actor, and William Shakespeare, the author, were one and the same. There were never any written testimonies to the contrary.

Will wrote historical plays from the beginning, following the same themes and patterns as other playwrights. *Henry VI, Part I* was written in 1590 and *Parts II* and *III* in 1591 and there is evidence they were staged in March of the following year at the Rose Theatre. Shakespeare was also acting in the same year and appeared in Ben Jonson's play *Every Man in his Humour*. In 1593 his retelling of the story of *Venus and Adonis* as a long narrative poem was published by his Stratford colleague, Richard Field, and the following year *The Rape of Lucrece* was published in the same vogue. He dedicated both works to a young nobleman called Henry Wriothesley, Earl of Southampton and Baron

Titchfield, of whom he had become very fond. Southampton was attracted to poets, actors and those in the theatre and helped sponsor some of Will's efforts. There was much re-writing of existing plays among playwrights of the day and plots were often lifted from earlier works. Shakespeare would have been no exception to this practice and, as a young actor busily learning his lines, rehearsing and performing new parts (a different play was performed every afternoon of the week), he must have been hard put to find the time to write original work.

London was infested by a great plague in 1592, during which time the government ordered the closure of all theatres. They were to remain shut until the summer of 1594, by which time five per cent of London's population had been wiped out. During the intervening period, most players went on tour around the country, but Will did not follow this course. Instead, he took to writing poetry and plays and may have returned to Stratford. It is thought that some of his earlier sonnets and love poems were written during this period. By now, Will realised his true vocation was to write for the theatre and, in particular, to incorporate his abilities as a poet into his works.

Every subject's duty is the King's; but every subject's soul is his own

Henry V, Act 4, Scene 1

When the Lord Chamberlain's Men were formed in 1597, Will became one of their leading lights as both an actor and playwright. The troupe's members included Richard Burbage, who had become the best-known tragic actor of the day (he was the son of James Burbage, one of the most influential people in Will's life), Augustine Phillips, Henry Condell and John Heminges, the latter two being responsible for collecting and publishing the *First Folio* in 1623.

A number of actors in this company were to become some of Shakespeare's closest allies, whom he would adhere to for the remainder of his life. They often met for bouts of drinking and conversation at the Mermaid tavern, which once stood on Bread Street, near its junction with Cheapside. Besides Shakespeare, the get-together comprised Christopher Marlowe, the Burbages, Ben Jonson and other members of the acting and literary fraternity. Another meeting place was the Mitre tavern, which was at the corner of Old Mitre Court near St Dunstan-in-the-West Church, in the area of Fleet Street.

During the 1590s, Shakespeare was living in the parish of St Helen, Bishopsgate (A6), in Shoreditch, situated outside the city wall close to the earliest theatres. Amongst the overwhelming high-rise office blocks which dominate the area today, the local parish church is still intact, despite war damage and the terrorist bombs of 1992–93. This building would have been known to Will, who most probably worshipped here.

St Helen's Church, Bishopsgate, London
Tel: 020 7283 2231

In the 14th century, the north aisle belonged to a convent of Benedictine nuns who, in 1385, were reproved for 'the number of little dogs kept by the prioress, kissing secular persons, and wearing ostentatious veils'. The church consists of two naves, divided by a row of arches with a screen between, separating the nuns from the parishioners. The building also has a plethora of handsome monuments such as that of Sir William Pickering, Queen Elizabeth's Ambassador to Spain, which is a magnificent marble tomb surrounded by a wrought-iron rail. Another Elizabethan, Sir Thomas Gresham (died 1579), is commemorated by a large but rather uninteresting tomb, on which his personal crest appears – an heraldic carving, topped by a grasshopper. He was the Queen's agent in the Low Countries, a man of letters, and one of Will's fellow parishioners at St Helen's. (Sir Thomas was also a successful financier who built and founded the original Royal Exchange, establishing it as a centre for commerce in 1565. It lay between Cornhill and Threadneedle Street. At the centre of the building was a vast courtyard where merchants and tradesmen did business. Elizabeth I bestowed its royal title and, to this day, the Royal Exchange is one of the sites from which a new monarch is proclaimed. The present structure dates from 1844, and it is now a high-class shopping complex.)

Another tomb in St Helen's is that of Sir John Crosby, an important dealer in the wool trade and head of a large grocery business. His house, Crosby Place, stood nearby. In the north wall of St Helen's is a striking stained-glass window depicting Shakespeare, which was presented in 1884 by H. H. Prentice of the USA. It was the only window to survive bomb damage. Unfortunately, much of the surrounding area of the church was re-developed in the 1880s, leaving no clues as to where Shakespeare actually lodged.

In spring, the Lord Chamberlain's Men usually performed at public venues, such as The Theatre, and went on tour around the country during summer months. They returned to London for the autumn season before finding sanctuary during the winter period at one or another of the local inns. There they rehearsed new material, especially plays which they were to present at court before the Queen during Christmas festivities. They regularly gave such performances, which allowed them an opportunity to fraternise with some of the nobility and other poets of the day who, in turn, frequented The Theatre. It was probably at such an event, while still with the Earl of Leicester's Men, that Shakespeare was introduced to the Earl of Southampton, his first sponsor. It was to prove a very fruitful meeting.

Doubt thou the stars are fire; doubt that the sun doth move;
Doubt truth to be a liar; but never doubt I love

Hamlet, Act 2, Scene 2

CHAPTER 7

The Globe Theatre

HENRY WRIOTTESLEY, 3rd Earl of Southampton and Baron Titchfield, was twenty when Shakespeare dedicated his first narrative poem to him – *Venus and Adonis*. It was published in 1593 by former Stratfordian, Richard Field, and was followed up the next year by a similar offering – *The Rape of Lucrece* – again dedicated to Southampton. By 1597, Will had been named as one of the Lord Chamberlain's Men and had already written a number of plays, including the three parts of *Henry VI, Richard III, Edward III, Titus Andronicus, The Comedy of Errors, The Taming of the Shrew, The Two Gentlemen of Verona, Love's Labour's Lost, Romeo and Juliet* and *Richard II*. He became a prolific playwright whose works were not only suitable for performing at many different types of venues but usually attracted large audiences. At the same time, his standing and stature as an actor had grown, and it is thought he had a fondness for playing 'Kingly' as well as character roles in various productions.

But what do we know of the Earl of Southampton? Firstly, he came from a Roman Catholic dynasty, in which his father had been a strong supporter of the old religion. Secondly, the family home was Titchfield Abbey (B4) near Fareham, Hampshire, which is now a ruin. Shakespeare may possibly have stayed there with his future patron, and also at his London home. The Hampshire property came into the family's possession from the Dissolution of the Monasteries. At the age of eight years, in 1581, at his father's death, Henry was made a ward of court and came under the care of William Cecil, Lord Burghley, the Queen's Lord Treasurer. From the age of twelve the boy was educated at Cambridge, where he gained a Master of Arts degree after four years. This led him to London, where he continued his studies at Gray's Inn, a school of law and kind of finishing school in social etiquette for society gentlemen.

By all accounts, Southampton was a good-looking youth, thought by some to be bisexual, and wore his hair in long curls – hardly the fashion of the day. By the time he met Shakespeare he had already gained favour with Queen Elizabeth, as his immense wealth had led him into both court and theatrical circles. In the latter he was able to

Mary Arden's House, Wilmcote

Palmer's Farm, Wilmcote

Holy Trinity Church, Stratford

Statue, Henley Street, Stratford

Anne Hathaway's Cottage, Shottery

Guildhall and site of New Place, Stratford

Kenilworth Castle

Charlecote Park, Warwickshire

Hall's Croft, Stratford

The Globe Theatre, Bankside, London

Royal Shakespeare Theatre, Stratford

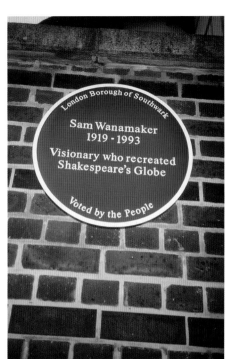

Sam Wanamaker's memorial plaque,
The Globe Theatre

The White Tower, Tower of London

Shakespeare's Birthday Celebrations, Stratford

sponsor the work of new playwrights, such as Will. It has been suggested that he and Shakespeare took a trip to Italy together around 1593, as settings for *The Two Gentlemen of Verona*, *Romeo and Juliet* and *The Merchant of Venice* are Italian, and all three plays were written within the space of a couple of years.

Southampton wanted to emulate the Queen's current favourite, Robert Devereux, Earl of Essex. Despite his upbringing at a Protestant court, he became involved in both political and religious intrigue, which soon led him into trouble. He was anxious to accompany Essex on a military expedition, rather than stay at home and marry in order to continue the family line and ensure the succession of his title. It was said that his own mother, or even Lord Burghley, invited Shakespeare to dedicate some of his sonnets to the fair gentleman, with a view to persuading him against leaving. The result was that Will wrote seventeen sonnets for private reading, with no intention of publishing them at the time. In the main, he addresses them to his 'lovely boy' or the 'beautiful young man' who steals away his mistress – a dark married woman – and then transfers his affections to another poet. This may suggest to some that Shakespeare had become emotionally involved with his patron. But if a flood of feelings had been released by the author, it does not necessarily mean that his relationship with Southampton was of a physical nature.

There is no specific clue as to the identity of the woman mentioned in the sonnets, but there is a supposition it could have been the wife of John Florio, an Italian scholar who was then acting as secretary to the Earl of Southampton.

When these sonnets were finally printed fifteen years later, the publisher added rather a puzzling dedication to a 'Mr W. H.'. Could this have been a reversal of the initials of Henry Wriottesley? Some have claimed that the youth in question was William Herbert, the future Earl of Pembroke. As it happens, he was only twelve when the sonnets were written by Shakespeare. His mother, the Lady Mary Herbert, was one of the great literary patrons of the day and she may have requested Shakespeare write the sonnets for her son's birthday.

William Herbert's birthplace was Wilton House (B2) near Salisbury. He went to Oxford at the age of twelve but left two years later to become a courtier to Queen Elizabeth. In 1601, he inherited the title of 3rd Earl of Pembroke, and later married the heiress of the 7th Earl of Shrewsbury. Like Southampton, he became a great benefactor of the arts, and gave his name to Pembroke College in Oxford. Pembroke was another of Shakespeare's sponsors and, according to tradition, he invited Will and his players to perform *As You Like It* in the Great Hall at Wilton House on 2 December 1603, before King James I. (In 1623, John Heminges and Henry Condell, publishers of the *First Folio* of Shakespeare's works, dedicated the collection to Pembroke and his brother, the Earl of Montgomery). The Earl of Pembroke died in London in 1630, and was buried in Salisbury Cathedral.

Wilton House, nr Salisbury
Tel: 01722 746729

The history of the site begins at the time of King Ecgbert in 838 AD, when a nunnery was founded. After the Dissolution, it was given by Henry VIII to the 1st Earl of Pembroke; another bequest from the King's ill-gotten gains. Pembroke demolished most of the abbey and, from its stones, built Wilton House as his family home. The house was destroyed by fire in 1647, and later rebuilt to the designs of Inigo Jones and John Webb. Its noble rooms house many famous paintings by artists such as Rubens, Rembrandt and Van Dyck.

Most of Shakespeare's later sonnets are dedicated to another mysterious Dark Lady. This figure is known to have been married and to have had a number of lovers, and various suggestions and theories have been put forward as to her true identity. One is that she was Emilia Lanier, an Italian Jewess, a woman of some substance who lived in London. However, many authors believe the Dark Lady was Lady Mary Fitton, the younger daughter of Sir Edward and Lady Alice Fitton. Lady Mary was born in 1578 at Gawsworth Hall (E14) near Macclesfield, Cheshire, and in 1596 was appointed one of Queen Elizabeth's Ladies-in-Waiting. But after a wild affair she was discovered to have become pregnant – by the same William Herbert, later 3rd Earl of Pembroke, believed to be the 'Mr W. H.' of the sonnets, who at that time had emerged as a prominent courtier. The couple were instantly dismissed from the Queen's service and detained at the Tower of London. Pembroke was seconded, for a term, to the Fleet Prison, while Lady Mary returned to her family home. Later, she became mistress to Admiral Sir Richard Leveson (his family lived at the Old Hall in Wolverhampton – now the site of the Central Library and Old Hall Street). In 1588, Leveson had led the small English fleet in its attack on the Spanish Armada. He later installed Lady Mary at a house in

Perton, South Staffordshire, where she bore him two children. He died in London in 1605, and his splendid bronze statue and memorial can be seen in the Lady Chapel of St Peter's Collegiate Church, Wolverhampton (E17), where he is interred. After his death, Lady Mary married twice – first to a Captain William Polewhele, by whom she had more children; then to a Mr Lougher, a landowner with property in England and Wales. She died in 1647 and her burial is recorded in the parish registers of St Michael and All Angels Church, Tettenhall (E17), now an attractive leafy suburb of Wolverhampton.

From the time of his writing *Venus and Adonis,* Shakespeare was to compose over 160 sonnets or poems and 40 plays. He became the best accomplished playwright of his day. Whoever the sonnets may be for, the works are Shakespeare's spiritual biography and from them emerges a profile of someone able to express every shade of passion – ranging from the platonic affection for a friend to the torments of jealousy; from the lighthearted to deep sorrow; and from sensual ecstasy to darkest repugnance. For years, students of Shakespeare have searched for clues to try and piece together the various aspects of his amorous nature or state of sensuality. Undoubtedly, if an early marriage in Stratford had restricted his true feelings, Will would have found more than ample opportunity for infidelity in London, amongst the loose living of his fellow writers, artistes and various members of the nobility. Shakespeare makes several references to his 'dark-eyed lady' in the sonnets and there are hints of his possible bisexuality. It is said that, occasionally, he had to seek out 'unwholesome' treatments from local doctors to counteract sexually transmitted diseases.

The Lord Chamberlain's Men provided Shakespeare with a period of stability during which he was able to write and perform. On average, he completed at least two plays a year. In 1597 the troupe of players were invited to provide all performances of plays before the Queen.

Friendship is constant in all other things
save in the office and affairs of love

> *Much Ado About Nothing*, Act 2, Scene 1

In August 1596, Will received the disturbing and unwelcome news from Stratford that his only son, Hamnet, was desperately ill. He may have been too late to see his son for a last time, or even to make it to the burial on 11 August. Hamnet was eleven years old when he died and Will was overcome with grief. It was undoubtedly a time for family reflection as he was re-united with his wife, Anne, two daughters, Susanna and Judith, parents, and other loved ones. It was about this time that Will assisted his father's discharge from bankruptcy. Soon after an application was made to the College of Arms, possibly with help from Will, and John was finally granted a coat of arms for his family on 20 October 1596. The motto on the arms was *Non Sanz Droit* which appropriately translates as 'Not Without Right' Alas, John Shakespeare had only a few years left to enjoy the privilege, and died in 1601. He did, however, manage to see his son become a phenomenal success as a poet, playwright and man of the theatre.

On John's death, the family home in Henley Street was bequeathed to Will, who allowed his mother and remaining family to continue living there. After his mother's death on 9 September 1608 he let the dwelling to his sister, Joan Hart, and her husband for a nominal rent. Meanwhile, the family business had probably been carried on in the eastern section of the house by Will's two unmarried brothers, Gilbert and Richard.

It is known that in November 1597 Shakespeare moved his place of lodging to a different address in the Bishopsgate area of London as he is listed as failing to pay a tax of five shillings before moving. On 1 October 1598 he was again wanted for tax evasion in the parish of St Helen's. This all seems somewhat out of character for a man who had started to earn a good income through his literary and acting abilities. Will had by then completed *A Midsummer Night's Dream* and *King John*. He continued writing with *The Merchant of Venice* and *Henry IV*, *Parts I* and *II*.

In 1597, when the lease on The Theatre ran out, and following a dispute with the landowner, Richard Burbage and his brother Cuthbert clandestinely supervised the dismantling of the old theatre building in Shoreditch. They built, mainly using materials rescued from the dismantled fabric, the famous theatre called the Globe. It was erected in the Bankside area, just south of the River Thames. It is said that at the time the Thames was frozen over, allowing timbers and other building materials to be carried across the ice. The alternative would have been to transport everything across London Bridge.

The theatre was octagonal in shape and built of seasoned wood, with angled joints and three galleries, and was supported by many pillars in stone and marble. In the centre was a platform stage, covered by a large decorative canopy which partly protected the actors from inclement weather. This facility allowed audiences to see and hear productions as clearly as possible. The play which opened the Globe theatre on 12

June 1599 was *As You Like It*, Shakespeare's latest work, although it was not officially registered by the Lord Chamberlain's Men until 4 August 1600. It was an instant success and the theatre provided Will with a venue to stage new works, while receiving a salary for acting in them and a percentage of the takings. Shakespeare later described the Globe as 'this wooden O' in the opening chorus of *Henry v*. Finance for the project was raised through an offer of shares to leading actors in the Lord Chamberlain's Men, including Shakespeare, who accepted the offer and had a stake of one tenth in the Globe theatre. Other financiers included John Heminges, Augustine Phillips, Tom Pope and the two Burbage brothers. In May 1599 an inventory of property belonging to Thomas Brend (father of the leaseholder of the land on which the Globe theatre stood) listed Will as occupying a new house in St Saviour's Parish. He had reached the age of 35 and his future as a playwright was assured.

Two of Will's brothers also fancied their chances in London. Gilbert Shakespeare, two years younger than Will, became a haber-dasher in the parish of St Bridget. He never married but maintained links with Stratford. The youngest brother, Edmund, born 1580, also became an actor but in no way enjoyed the success of his eldest brother. He fathered an illegitimate son, who died in infancy and was buried at St Giles Church Without Cripplegate (A4) in August 1607. In the following December Edmund also died, and was interred at St Saviour's Church, Bankside (now Southwark Cathedral) on 31 December 1607. The ceremony was held in the morning in order to allow actors to perform in the afternoon. William Shakespeare paid for both funerals.

Southwark Cathedral, London
Tel: 020 7367 6700

The cathedral church covering the Bankside area, in the borough of Southwark, stands in a prominent position close to London Bridge, overlooking the Thames from the south bank. A church in Southwark was first mentioned in the Domesday Book, and built on an earlier Saxon site. After 1066 it became the priory church of St Mary Overie, and it was severely damaged by fire in 1212. It was rebuilt in the Early English style. After the Dissolution in 1539 the priory was designated the parish church of St Saviour. In 1611, the parishioners bought the building from King James 1 for £800 and, with it, the option of appointing their own minister. It was once in the diocese of Winchester but, in 1905, a new diocese of Southwark was created, and the church elevated to the status of a cathedral. It is one of the few sites in modern London which Shakespeare would recognise. Edmund Shakespeare's tombstone can be seen in the floor of the Choir, and two former members of the King's Men are buried nearby. These are John Fletcher, dramatist (1579–1625), who died during a plague, and Philip Massinger, dramatist (1583–1639).

Other Bankside actors and men of the theatre were associated with this church, including Philip Henslowe – proprietor of the Rose theatre; and Edward Alleyn – who became a vestryman. Not the least to be commemorated in the Cathedral is William Shakespeare himself, in a fine memorial and window situated at the east end of the south aisle. The memorial depicts Shakespeare in a restful position in Bankside, set against background images of St Saviour's Church, Winchester Palace, and the Globe and Rose theatres. The memorial was designed by Henry McCarthy in 1911. Above is the Shakespeare Window, which includes images of various characters depicted in Will's plays. During the 19th century a series of stained glass windows by Kemp portrayed the works of various Elizabethan dramatists. Sadly, these were destroyed in 1940 by a bomb which fell in the nearby Borough Market. The replacement window was designed by Christopher Webb in 1954 and unveiled by actress Dame Sybil Thorndike, well-known for her portrayal of Shakespearean roles. It is appropriate that, to the right of the Memorial, there is a commemorative tablet to the American actor and director Sam Wanamaker (1913–1993). He masterminded the building of the new Shakespeare's Globe nearby, which was completed in 1997. Sam had a dream of re-building the Globe as near as possible to its original site and design. It was sad that he never lived long enough to see his dream come to fruition!

By coincidence, in 1607 a certain John Harvard was baptised at St Saviour's and Shakespeare is said to have attended the service. Harvard was to become the main benefactor of the first college to be established in America, in 1638 – Harvard College in Massachusetts. His father owned a butcher's shop, close to St Saviour's, and the Queen's Head Inn, on the site of the present 103 Borough High Street. His father and four of his brothers and sisters died of the plague, which swept London in 1625. John's mother died ten years later, bequeathing to her son the Queen's Head, a part share in a house on Tower Hill, and an amount of money. Two years later, his surviving brother died, making John Harvard the sole beneficiary of the family properties and monies.

Harvard House, Stratford (SH)
Tel: 01789 204016

John became a clergyman and married Katherine Rogers, daughter of a master butcher, Thomas Rogers. The Rogers were known to the Shakespeares as they once owned a house in High Street, Stratford-upon-Avon. It is a lovely black and white half-timbered house, built 1598 and named Harvard House (c5). The building stands diagonally across from the Town Hall and boasts an ornately carved, timber-framed frontage. Over recent years, it has become home to the Museum of British Pewter. The exhibition illustrates the history of 2,000 years of British pewter, and displays also relate to the life of John Harvard. He emigrated to America in 1637, and took with him about four hundred books – most of them being of an academic nature. Sadly, John died of consumption at the age of thirty in 1638. In his will was a bequest to Harvard College of £1,700 together with a large stock of books. This led to the founding of a new college in Cambridge on the outskirts of Boston, Massachusetts. It subsequently became Harvard University.

John Harvard is also commemorated in Southwark Cathedral in the Harvard Chapel, which contains some of the earliest surviving masonry within the church. The chapel was restored in his memory in 1907 by the Sons and Friends of Harvard University, on the initiative of William Phillips. The east window in the chapel was the gift of Joseph H. Choate, the American Ambassador to Britain between 1899–1905. To the right of the chapel entrance is a memorial tablet to Oscar Hammerstein, the American lyricist, who left a bursary to be spent in the training of two choristers – to be known as the Hammerstein Chanters. The nearby tower staircase leads up to the belfry, once visited by Charles Dickens, who wrote about his experience in *Household Words* (1850).

George Inn, Southwark, London (NT)
Tel: 020 7407 2056

The main road from London to the south crossed over London Bridge and continued on Long Southwark. It is known today as Borough High Street, and many famous inns and hostelries were once situated there – such as the Bell, the Tabard, the White Hart and the George (A18). The last-named lies through an alleyway off the main street and the galleries of this famous inn once ranged round at least three sides of the courtyard. Such places, offering a good view for spectators on upper levels, were suitable for public performances of plays and other forms of entertainment. This hostelry is typical of the sort of environment where Shakespeare and his players would have performed when on tour, and it is known the Bard was familiar with the inn's hospitality. The site was a well-known coaching inn during the 17th century and is referred to by Charles Dickens in his novel *Little Dorrit*, much of which is set within the parish of Southwark. Today, the George Inn is administered by The National Trust, leased to a private company, but still in use as a public house.

New Place, Stratford (SH)

Tel: 01789 292325

With his new found wealth, William Shakespeare decided on a more opulent home in Stratford where he and his family could live. Up to that time, his wife and their two daughters had lived in Henley Street. They moved to the much larger New Place (C7) at the corner of Chapel Street and Chapel Lane. It was a 15th century mansion, which Will bought from a William Underhill on 4 May 1597. The dwelling was originally built in 1483 by Sir Hugh Clopton, and was Stratford's second largest house and the first to be built of brick. It stood in extensive grounds, just opposite the Guild Chapel and Will's old grammar school. New Place was a five-gabled, three-storeyed house, fronting onto Chapel Street, with exterior buildings grouped around a courtyard. At the centre was a well, which has survived, together with cellars and foundations uncovered in later years. The property had two gardens and orchards, which are mentioned in the house deeds. When not on occasional visits to London, Shakespeare would have resided here in a form of retirement from about 1610 up to the time of his death in 1616. It would have provided some form of stability for the family, whatever the marital relationship might have become between Anne and Will. It is quite possible that some of his later manuscripts were written at his final home.

New Place was virtually demolished before rebuilding was undertaken by John Clopton, around 1702. A later owner, the Reverend Francis Gastrell – frustrated by the intrusion on his privacy by countless visitors and sightseers – had a mulberry tree, thought to have been planted in his garden by Shakespeare, chopped down. At a later date, in 1759, this clergyman had the house demolished. This act of folly so angered the local townsfolk that he was forced to leave Stratford. Today, the area that remains is occupied by attractive garden space, including a knot garden based on an Elizabethan design. During Spring and summer months, this area is a riot of colour, carefully contained within the four 'knots'. This section occupies the former site of the main house. (As at Shakespeare's Birthplace, many plants mentioned in his works have been planted.) Beyond is the Great Garden, which is reached from Chapel Lane. It contains box and yew hedges, borders, flower beds, lawns and an old mulberry tree, possibly grown from a cutting from the original planted by Shakespeare.

Like madness is the glory of this life

> *Timon of Athens*, Act 1, Scene 2

It is believed that in 1602 the first performance of *Twelfth Night* was given by the Lord Chamberlain's Men in the splendid Middle Temple Hall (A10). Queen Elizabeth was entertained there, along with her sea dogs, Drake and Frobisher. The present building was erected in the 1560s and provided the setting for many Elizabethan plays and masques. It can be visited by the public, who are able to see the excellent hammer beam roof, wooden panelling and decorative screen. Middle Temple is situated between the Victoria Embankment and Fleet Street and is one of the Inns of Court. Another nearby venue is Gray's Inn, the setting for the first performance of *The Comedy of Errors* in 1594. It is situated on the north side of South Street, and was built between 1556–60.

Due to the success of the Globe, other theatres began to mushroom in London. Philip Henslowe and Edward Alleyn – Richard Burbage's great rival as the outstanding actor of the day – must have realised the advent of the Globe gave a distinct advantage to the Lord Chamberlain's Men over their own Admiral's Men, who performed at the nearby Rose theatre. Consequently, in competition, they built a new theatre at Cripplegate in Shoreditch, named the Fortune. It was about half a mile to the west of the existing Curtain theatre, but far enough away from competition at Bankside, south of the river. The Admiral's Men moved to the Fortune in 1600, whilst the vacated Rose was leased to the Earls of Worcester's and Pembroke's Men. In 1602, Worcester's Men moved to the Curtain theatre, and joined a combination of Pembroke's Men and Oxford's Men to form a third principal theatre company.

One of the earliest plays to be produced at the Globe theatre was

Shakespeare's *Julius Caesar*. The timing of this play was rather unfortunate as his sponsor, the Earl of Southampton, was by then deeply involved with the Earl of Essex in an unsuccessful coup d'état against the Queen. Essex was executed, whilst Southampton was condemned to the Tower in 1601 for supporting the rebellion.

Although Will wrote *The Merry Wives of* Windsor in 1602, Elizabeth's final years brought about a form of depression across the nation which was reflected in the mood of some of Will's plays such as *Hamlet* and *Troilus and Cressida*. The Queen died at Richmond Palace on 24 March 1603 and James VI, son of Mary Queen of Scots, was proclaimed King James I of England, thus uniting the two kingdoms of England and Scotland under one ruler – a lifetime ambition of Henry VIII.

The start of a new reign brought about a new enthusiasm and King James soon became patron of the Lord Chamberlain's Men. From then on, they changed their name to the King's Men. However, despite the re-grouping of theatre companies, one of the greatest threats to the King's Men came from the resurgence of children's companies, such as the boys of St Paul's Cathedral Choir and the Chapel Royal. Both had performed at court and at a theatre in Blackfriars (A8). These young people were supported by prominent writers such as Ben Jonson and John Marston, who wrote material for the children, and in return received public performances of their works. But the popularity of these child performers was only short-lived and soon no longer posed a threat to adult theatre companies.

The main shareholders of the Globe theatre were given honorary titles by King James as Grooms of the Royal Bedchamber. The new king, like Elizabeth, became an enthusiastic supporter of the theatre and of work written by the new wave of playwrights. However, there was a setback to London theatre life when another plague raged through the city between 1603 and 1604 and, once again, theatres were closed down. The King set off on a royal progress through parts of his enlarged kingdom and theatrical performances were given in his honour at some of the great houses and palaces where he stayed. Despite the lack of theatre life in London, Shakespeare soon became a great favourite of King James. It was to lead to even greater success.

Let's make us med'cines of our great revenge
To cure this deadly grief

Macbeth, Act 4, Scene 3

CHAPTER 8

The King's Men

KING JAMES HAD only been in London ten days when he adopted the Lord Chamberlain's Men under his own patronage as the King's Men. This acknowledged them as the leading company of the day, which must have upset some of the others who had made names for themselves and their activities. As a member of the King's Men, Shakespeare was appointed an ex-officio Groom of the Bedchamber, and was entitled to four and a half yards of scarlet cloth to use as his livery at the forthcoming coronation. (This was held in the spring but was a much scaled-down affair due to the outbreak of plague in the metropolis. Shakespeare marched in the procession through London in his scarlet robes.) Will was only second in line in the list of members on the King's Men's royal patent. The first was Lawrence Fletcher, who had been the King's favourite player in Scotland. The royal patent protected the King's Men against harassment by the London City fathers, and entitled them to play 'within their now usual house of the Globe.' King James took absolute control of drama, limiting the number of companies to three – the King's Men, Prince Henry's (the Prince of Wales) Men and Queen Anne's Men – and royal patents also allowed these three bodies to perform in provincial centres.

It was really from 1601 onwards that Shakespeare started to write major tragedies – *Hamlet, Othello, King Lear, Macbeth, Anthony and Cleopatra* and *Coriolanus* (the last-named completed in 1607). The actor Thomas Pope died in the summer of 1603 and three more actors were brought in to become King's Men. These were Nicholas Tooley and Alexander Cook – both had already worked their apprenticeship as actors – and John Lowin, a large gentleman with a commanding presence who excelled in roles such as Falstaff and Henry VIII. In August the troupe were invited to appear before the Spanish Ambassador at Somerset House, and during the autumn the King witnessed no fewer than twelve performances, eight of which were plays by Shakespeare. He saw *Othello* at the Banqueting House (A13) of Whitehall Palace on the first of November; *The Merry Wives of Windsor* on the fourth. *Measure for Measure* – the final comedy to be written by Shakespeare

– was performed on Christmas Day. Two days later, *The Comedy of Errors* was staged. Furthermore, at the following Shrovetide, the King commanded two consecutive performances of *The Merchant of Venice*.

The King's Men soon found themselves on a tour of aristocratic mansions and royal palaces, appearing wherever the court happened to be in residence. As well as Whitehall, there were the Palaces of Greenwich, Richmond, Hampton Court and Windsor Castle. Each of these places acted as the backdrop to a scene in one or more of Shakespeare's plays. During the time between James's accession and Shakespeare's death, the troupe were invited to perform at court on no fewer than 187 occasions.

Bubonic plague again ravaged London in 1604, when Shakespeare is known to have moved back north of the river to Silver Street, Cripplegate, where he resided with Christopher and Mary Mountjoy. This street was the hub of the lucrative wig industry and the couple, of French descent, were headdress and wig-makers. It is thought that, whilst lodging with the Mountjoys, Shakespeare started to write *Othello*, in which he showcased the dramatic prose of his comedies and histories, perfected in *Measure for Measure* and *Hamlet*. Will Shakespeare had, by then, reached the pinnacle of his career. Between November 1604 and February 1605, the King's Men presented at least seven of his plays at court – *Othello, The Merry Wives of Windsor, Measure for Measure, The Comedy of Errors, Love's Labour's Lost, Henry* V and *The Merchant of Venice* – and gave two performances of Ben Jonson's comedies. In order to flatter King James, Shakespeare delved into Scottish history, as depicted in Holinshed's *Chronicles*, and wrote *Macbeth*. It was given its first performance before the King at Hampton Court Palace in August 1606. Banquo was an ancestor of James and Shakespeare portrays him kindly in the play, with a prophetic vision of James's own rule over the two newly-united kingdoms.

> *How far that little candle throws his beams!*
> *So shines a good deed in a naughty world*
>
> > *The Merchant of Venice*, Act 2, Scene 1

Meanwhile, in Stratford, domestic and family events had been taking place. In May 1607, Will's elder daughter, Susanna, was reprimanded for having broken the law by her absence from Sacrament the previous Easter – but the case was dismissed. In the following month, aged 24, she married Dr John Hall, a young Stratford physician, who had made quite a name for himself. He obtained his degree at Cambridge and probably initially practised medicine abroad. John followed in his father William Hall's footsteps – he also practised medicine (though many of his theories were based on astrology). John Hall was a skilled herbalist and a number of his cures proved to have positive effects on his patients. As Shakespeare was nearing his forty-fourth birthday he was given the news that, in February 1608, he had become a grandfather. Susanna gave birth to a baby girl, Elizabeth, after only eight months of marriage. (Perhaps she and John Hall had married under the same circumstances as her parents had done?) Will's mother, Mary Arden, managed to see her first great-grandchild before she died, aged 68, in the following September. This event most likely brought Shakespeare back to Stratford to attend the funeral and burial service at Holy Trinity Church.

Shakespeare held the Hall family in high regard and eventually left New Place to Susanna in his will. John had already acquired a comfortable living and could afford a spacious house of his own, now known as Hall's Croft (C11), at Old Town near to Holy Trinity Church, Stratford. It was originally a Tudor building until the main part of the house was enlarged in Jacobean style in 1613, probably to include a dispensary and consulting room. Meanwhile, Will's remaining daughter Judith and his wife Anne continued to reside at New Place. After Will's death in 1616, the Halls moved into New Place and remained there until John's own death in 1635.

Hall's Croft, Stratford (SH)

Tel: 01789 292107

After the Halls left the house, the half-timbered building was owned by a range of professional people and served as a small school in the mid-19th century. Hall's Croft was bought by the Shakespeare Birthplace Trust in 1949 and they restored and furnished the house as it might have appeared when occupied by the Hall family.

On entering the house, the stone-flagged entrance hall and parlour are spacious, dominated by a large stone fireplace and 17th century panel-back armchairs. Of particular interest are an ornate child's high chair made of ash, and an armchair of yew – perfect examples of furniture of the Jacobean period. The visitor then passes from the parlour, with its excellent central draw leaf 17th century table furniture and an eye-catching large Dutch painting of *A Family Saying Grace Before A Meal*, and enters a passageway which has a view of the garden from a small window. Noticeable is a mid-17th century bookbinding press, together with a portrait of one of Dr Hall's contemporaries, Michael Drayton, whom he once treated for a fever.

The next room was the consulting area, where a range of items depict a typical doctor's surgery, with a collection of drug jars arranged on shelving. Two more Dutch paintings depict a patient in consultation with his doctor and an apothecary about his work. Various medical items are displayed in a wall cupboard with fine parquetry work, including some English delft jars once used for the storage of medicine and ointments. From this room a few steps lead down to a back hall, in which sits a large wooden 17th century mural cupboard, plus a seat-table with a hinged top and a storage compartment below.

Moving into the kitchen, we see a large fireplace and cooking utensils, together with a spit assembly of wrought iron with a drip pan underneath. Other cooking utensils and various implements for the spit are hung on the wall above. At the foot of a staircase is a 1627 portrait by Nicolaes Eliasz of Amsterdam of a *Mother and Child*, and ascending to the first floor we discover a landing with another painting of the English School, circa 1570, entitled *Death and the Maiden*.

We now enter the principal barrel-vaulted bedroom which has a bed, a hinged-top stool depicting the sanitary arrangements of the period, a clothes press with fine carvings, a cupboard with ventilation panels, and a beautifully-carved chest which sits beneath the window. The portrait, completed in 1620, is of Mary Harvey, a relative of Dr William Harvey, another physician whom John Hall greatly respected. Sadly, the subject of the portrait died only two years after it was completed. At the corner of this bedchamber is a door which leads into a long chamber, once divided into bedrooms, where an exhibition recalls Dr John Hall's career and his theories about medicines of the day. There is a first edition of his famous casebook, *Select Observations on English Bodies*, first published in 1657, two years after his death. (His case-books were not published until they had been translated from the Latin.) Another door leads to a bedroom, furnished as a servant's room, in a simple style with period bed and stool. We then move along a passage-way – giving good views across the garden – back to the landing and staircase.

A door from the back hall opens into a walled garden. This plot of land must have been productive when Dr Hall and Susanna lived here, for many of the remedies used for the treatment of patients would have been created with fresh herbs from the garden. A formal herb garden has been maintained, and those items mentioned in Dr Hall's medical notebooks are still tended. Elsewhere, flowering plants sweep alongside the path, leading to a sundial and small arbour.

There is no doubt that some part of Shakespeare's own wealth of medical knowledge must have been derived through his relationship with John Hall. When Dr Hall died, nineteen years after Will, he also was interred in Holy Trinity Parish Church, close to his father-in-law. He was described as *medicus peritissimus* – a skilled medical practioner. In his will, Dr Hall bequeathed his money and possessions to be equally divided between his wife, Susanna, and daughter, Elizabeth, and gave his 'study of books' to his son-in-law, Thomas Nash, a wealthy local property owner.

Some rise by sin, and some by virtue fall

Measure for Measure, Act 2, Scene 1

When Elizabeth married Thomas Nash in 1626, it is thought they went to live with her parents at New Place. Nash owned the property next door, now known as Nash's House, and when he died in 1647 he left the property to his wife; it remained in her possession until her own death in 1670. They did not produce any children and Elizabeth was to be Shakespeare's last direct descendant. Although she re-married, to John Barnard in 1649, there was still no issue. The couple later moved to the Barnard family home in Northamptonshire.

Though New Place was demolished in the 18th century, the site is entered by the adjacent Nash's House. It is most appropriate, as both properties were strongly linked through family ownership. At various times in the past, the Great Garden of New Place belonged to Nash's House and, in turn, some of the latter's garden became part of the New Place estate. The furniture and artefacts on display in Nash's House are representative of what would have been familiar to both houses during the time of the Shakespeare family's residence of the properties.

Nash's House, Stratford (SH)

Tel: 01789 292325

Entering Nash's House, the visitor steps into the hall, which has some ornately-carved furniture, including chests and cupboards for storing documents. These were commissioned in 1594 by Stratford town council. There is a striking portrait of Joyce Clopton, descendant of Sir Hugh Clopton, the Stratford-born benefactor who built New Place and bequeathed so much to the town. The hall is spacious and leads to the parlour and kitchen areas. The parlour was once divided into two rooms, with a fireplace at either end. Here there is a richly decorated dining table and an open-shelved court cupboard with inlaid floral pattern, used for displaying plates and ceramic jars. Beyond is the small kitchen, furnished in the style of the 19th century, including a bread oven, plates, and other utensils.

Moving to the upper floor, the visitor may be surprised to find it is not furnished, as is the style with other Shakespeare Houses owned by the Trust, but is used for museum purposes. The first room contains a number of archaeological discoveries connected with Stratford's origins and history. Other rooms depict the town through various periods, including the Elizabethan and Jacobean eras; the background to the site of New Place; and samples of souvenirs carved from the mulberry tree said to have been planted by Shakespeare, removed from the garden in 1756. In a further room are some most interesting documents connected with Stratford's first Shakespeare Festival, held in 1769, and arranged by the famous actor, David Garrick. From this point, the visitor enters the adjacent garden and site of New Place.

Will's second daughter, Judith, was married rather late in life on 10 February 1616, at the age of 31. Her bridegroom was Thomas Quiney, son of Will's old Stratfordian colleague, Richard Quiney. They foolishly married during Lent, and Thomas was summoned to appear before the ecclesiastical court at Worcester, but failed to turn up. As a result, the couple was excommunicated. Quiney was five years junior to Judith and, a month after the wedding, admitted to earlier having had illicit sex with a local girl and making her pregnant. She had just died in childbirth, along with her infant. Quiney was put on trial, confessed, and was ordered to make public penance. He and Judith had three sons, but all died young.

Only the collateral line of Joan Shakespeare, one of Will's younger sisters, had any surviving descendents. She was married in the late 1590s to William Hart, a hatter from Stratford. Her eldest son, William, like his uncle Will, became an actor, but did not have any legitimate descendant. However, the fifth descendant of Joan's youngest son, Michael, became a furniture maker in Tewkesbury, and established the line of the Shakespeare-Hart family, which has survived.

> *Look, he's winding up the watch of his wit;*
> *Bye and bye it will strike*

> *The Tempest*, Act 2, Scene 1

Around 1608, the main juvenile group of players in London, known as the Children of the Revels, were undergoing problems. In August, their manager decided to relinquish the use of the Blackfriars Theatre to its owners, the Burbage family. In turn, the Burbages formed a group of seven 'house-keepers' – including Shakespeare, Heminges and Condell – to oversee the running of the building. This was of great benefit to the King's Men, as they now had another playhouse north of the river, which could be used as winter premises for performing plays. It also served a much wider cross-section of the theatre-going public than the Globe which, by and large, was supported by the upper classes, gentry and, sometimes, royalty. The problem with the Globe was that it was an open-topped theatre, very cold and windy in winter, in which an audience could include up to three thousand people, half of whom stood in the yard to watch performances. On the other hand, the Blackfriars Theatre was much more intimate and, though it could only hold up to 700, all could be seated in a much warmer environment.

Shareholders included Shakespeare, the Burbages, Heminges, Condell, William Sly and another, who represented one of the former leaseholders, Henry Evans. The lease for the Blackfriars theatre was signed in 1608. Romance was popular with its audiences and plays such as *The Two Gentlemen of Verona, A Midsummer Night's Dream* and *As You Like It* would have suited their tastes. (The former site of the theatre is now Playhouse Yard, just a short walk from the Blackfriars Bridge traffic intersection, crossing Queen Victoria Street and heading up an alleyway known as Blackfriars, turning right for Playhouse Yard (A8).) It all once formed part of a large Dominican monastery with inhabitants known as Black Friars, due to the colour of their habits. It is from these monks that the area takes its name. After the Dissolution, the monastery was rented out as apartments, houses and shops. The monastic buildings once covered the area from Puddle Dock, by the river, to Shoe Lane, off Fleet Street. A series of small alleys remain, which Shakespeare would have been familiar with. He later bought a property, once a priory gatehouse, in nearby Ireland Yard (the Cockpit pub is situated more or less on this site), which overlooked St Ann's Churchyard and another of the former monastic buildings, Provincial's Hall. Today, a section of the wall of the former monastery can be seen in those parts of the churchyard which still remain.

It was about this time that Shakespeare, on completion of the tragedies *Coriolanus* and *Anthony and Cleopatra* in 1608, decided to revisit the idea of writing romance. Taking his young granddaughter, Elizabeth Hall, as the model for the young heroine, Marina, he completed *Pericles* in the same year.

Plague spread through London again in 1609, and Shakespeare probably spent most of his time back at New Place in Stratford. It could have given him thoughts of retirement, but he is believed to have postponed the idea for another twelve months. This proved futile as the plague continued to take its toll and theatres were closed down. (Though they had been written earlier, it was in 1609 that Shakespeare's *Sonnets* were published, possibly issued without his consent.) By the following year, Shakespeare was 46 and had given up acting. He decided to vacate his London accommodation and retreat to Stratford, where he was able to complete *Cymbeline*. Soon afterwards, the dreaded epidemic began to subside, and Will probably spent as much time as ever in London with his company.

Shakespeare purchased a gatehouse in Blackfriars in 1613, and the transaction was witnessed by John Jackson, owner of the Mermaid tavern. The reason for the purchase remains a mystery – perhaps Will lived there for a period – but it had long been known to the authorities as a safe house where the Roman Catholic mass was celebrated. It is said that it had secret passages leading from the cellar to the nearby Thames. These would have provided a means of escape for recusant worshippers. Perhaps Will, like his father, still harboured leanings towards the old religion. In his will, the property was left to his daughter, Susanna, but with no specific instructions. A year or two later, the property was passed to two trustees of Shakespeare's will, Matthew Morris and John Greene. The mystery remains.

Will continued to produce more manuscripts and, as well as *The Winter's Tale*, he introduced *The Tempest*. Shortly afterwards, The King's Men took on two young writers, Francis Beaumont and John Fletcher, who had once written for the children who performed at

Blackfriars theatre. Beaumont collaborated with Fletcher, but had ceased to write for the theatre even before Shakespeare retired. Fletcher, however, collaborated with Will in the writing of *Henry VIII* in 1613. In the following year they wrote two more – *Cardenio* (a play since lost), and *The Two Noble Kinsmen*. Each of these later plays was presented at the Globe and at court.

> *In nature's infinite book of secrecy*
> *A little I can read*
>
> > *Anthony and Cleopatra*, Act 1, Scene 2

Mention must be made of the various tours made by the King's Men to locations across England during the reign of James I. These performances are more likely to have taken place during spring and summer months, during daylight hours, in a variety of venues, both indoor and outdoor. Certain towns were visited on a regular basis and a possible circuitous tour route from London could have included Ipswich (E26), Cambridge, Coventry, Stratford, Stafford (E15), Shrewsbury (E16), Bath (B19), and Oxford, where they would have arrived as Michaelmas began the new fiscal year. They perhaps moved on to the West Country before heading back to London. In addition, there would be stops and detours along the way to play at other towns and venues where they had been invited to perform by a local mayor or bailiff. Records are incomplete of actual dates and locations visited but those available do indicate some of the movements of Shakespeare's group of players. Let us take a look at some of the more important centres where performances took place.

Ipswich

Tel: 01473 258070 – TIC

As London was the main base of the King's Men, they may well have travelled through Maldon (B15) and Colchester to reach Ipswich. In Maldon, Essex, they would have performed at the Moot Hall, which was acquired in 1576 and still survives in part. Their venue in Ipswich may have been the council chamber of the ancient Moot Hall, situated on Cornhill, formerly the site of a Saxon market. King John granted the town its first charter in 1200. During the reign of Edward III weavers and wool workers from the Netherlands settled in the area and the

Suffolk wool industry grew rapidly. In 1518, Henry VIII granted a charter confirming the corporation's jurisdiction over the Orwell estuary.

In the Butter Market is the Ancient House, dated 1567, with a fine example of ornamentally carved plasterwork. Wolsey's Gateway (1528) is the only remaining fragment of the cardinal's plan to found a college at Ipswich; a town which has many medieval churches.

After leaving Ipswich, the players' route might have been westwards through Hadleigh, Sudbury and Haverhill, on the way to Cambridge. In Hadleigh (E25), the company are likely to have performed in the 15th century Guildhall, which still stands in a remarkable state of preservation, retaining many original features. At Sudbury, they may well have presented plays in the 14th century Moot Hall in Cross Street, or else its 16th century replacement – now demolished – on Market Hill.

Cambridge

Tel: 01223 322640 – TIC

Ben Jonson's *Volpone* was presented by the King's Men in Cambridge during the years 1605-07 as part of their tours. Unlike Oxford, the Cambridge university authorities discouraged theatrical groups, whom they considered rogues and vagabonds. On occasion they were given money not to perform in the town. The usual place of performance in Cambridge would have been the Guildhall, most probably at the invitation of the local mayor and corporation.

The city had been an important market town for The Fens long before the university was established. The earliest known settlement dates from Roman times; what is today the market place was once the site of Saxon settlements. In 1068, shortly after the Norman Conquest, the Normans built a castle near the old Roman site. According to the Domesday Book, there were about 400 houses in Cambridge by 1086. The settlement first came to real prominence in 1209 when a number of scholars moved there from Oxford and it became a centre of learning. By the mid-13th century, Cambridge was firmly established and recognised as a university city, with its own Chancellor. The first college, Peterhouse, was founded in 1284 by the Bishop of Ely, and during the next two centuries eleven more were founded. Today, it has more than thirty colleges. Pride of place must surely go to King's College, founded in 1440, which houses the magnificently pinnacled King's College Chapel, built in three stages between 1446 and 1515. The last stage included the wonderful Perpendicular fan-vaulted ceiling. The stained glass in the chapel is the most complete set of Renaissance windows to survive in any church in England.

Coventry
Tel: 02476 227264

In 1043 the Mercian Earl, Leofric, began Coventry's development as a centre for industry and commerce when he selected the small Saxon township as the site for a Benedictine monastery to replace a nunnery destroyed by the Danes. He donated land to the monks on which to raise their sheep, laying the foundation for the wool trade on which Coventry prospered for the next five hundred years. By 1400, Coventry ranked with Plymouth, Bristol and York as one of the leading provincial centres of England. Part of its wealth came from its cloth and thread, dyed blue by a special process which kept the colour from fading. 'True as Coventry blue', later 'true blue', became a byword for reliability. In 1642 the city refused admission to Charles I, and throughout the Civil War it was a Parliamentary stronghold. Royalists captured in the Midlands were imprisoned in the 14th century Church of St John in the Bablake area – 'sent to Coventry', as stated in an account dated 1647. After the restoration of the monarchy in 1660, the city was ordered to demolish its walls. Twelve gates were left, two of which survive today at either end of Lady Herbert's Garden.

The King's Men played regularly in Coventry, twice during 1603, when on their second visit they were paid the princely sum of twenty shillings for their efforts. This was the year of King James's accession. It was a town already known to Will from his youth, when he visited with his father to see the cycle of mystery plays performed by craft guilds. It is generally agreed by historians that the King's Men would have performed in St Mary's Guildhall on Bayley Lane, which runs on the south side of the ruins of the former Coventry Cathedral. The outer porch, with its 15th century gates, leads through to a courtyard. It is from here that visitors enter the complex, which includes an impressive great hall dating from the early 15th century. Dominating the north wall is a fine late 15th century stained glass window, depicting actual or legendary rulers of England, from the Roman Emperor Constantine and King Arthur to Henry V and Henry VI. Other rooms include the old council chamber and Prince's chamber. St Mary's Guildhall has stood for over 650 years and served as the centre of Henry VI's court during the Wars of the Roses, and, for a short time, as a prison for Mary Queen of Scots. It was built for the merchant Guild of St Mary, which later merged with others to form the powerful Trinity Guild, which counted Sir Richard (Dick) Whittington, Lord Mayor of London, amongst its members. In 1345 the Charter of Incorporation granted the city the right to have a mayor and, from then on, St Mary's Hall has been at the centre of the city's government. One item of furniture on view is a large oak table which was purchased from the Lucy family in 1902 for twenty pounds. Supposedly it was on this table that Sir Thomas Lucy signed William Shakespeare's arrest warrant for poaching deer at Charlecote. Shakespeare set a scene in *Henry VI, Part III* in the city; it depicts the Earl of Warwick walking on the walls with the Mayor of Coventry and others. Another scene, in *Richard II*, takes place in Coventry.

Stafford

Tel: 01785 619619 – TIC

Shakespeare's troupe, the King's Men, performed in Stafford in 1610 and 1613, being paid the fee of ten shillings on both occasions. A charming county town on the River Sow, Stafford was listed as a borough in the Domesday Book, and has a history which dates from before the Norman Conquest. The original Stafford Castle was built around 1350, but mostly destroyed in 1643 during the Civil War. It was rebuilt during the early 19th century. Stafford retains its medieval street pattern, built around the ancient market square, and some fine half-timbered houses remain. The most impressive is the many-gabled Ancient High House in Greengate Street, which sheltered Charles I and Prince Rupert for three nights in 1642. The parish church of St Mary lost much of its medieval stone when it was restored in the 1840s, but retains its 13th century nave, tower, and a fine Norman font. Izaac Walton (1593-1683), author of *The Compleat Angler*, was born in Eastgate Street and baptised in St Mary's, and is commemorated by a bust in the north aisle.

At the end of Elizabeth I's reign, Stafford was a small market town of about 1,500 inhabitants. The King's Men would have performed, at the invitation of the town's bailiff, in the Shire Hall. The old hall had been replaced – work began on the new building at the corner of the present Market Square and Greengate Street in 1587, and was completed in 1607. It was primarily a stone building. The final stage of construction included a checker pattern modelled on that at Warwick. It consisted of a hall supported on colonnades, the open space below being paved, and was used for assizes as well as meetings of county justices and other public events. There is documentary evidence that various troupes of actors performed in the town. By 1790, the Shire Hall was in a bad state of repair. Work began on a new building, designed by John Harvey, which was completed by 1798.

Shrewsbury

Tel: 01743 281200 – TIC

It is quite probable the acting company travelled from Stratford-upon-Avon to reach Shrewsbury. They may have gone via Henley-in-Arden (where they could have played at the Market House or Town Hall, demolished 1793), across the Forest of Arden, on to Bromsgrove, and westwards to Bewdley. They would then have turned north to follow the banks of the River Severn to Bridgnorth, the first river crossing, and on to Shrewsbury.

The King's Men visited Shrewsbury, close to the border of England and Wales, on four occasions between 1603 and 1613. Shakespeare had already written *Henry IV, Part 1,* which included the Battle of Shrewsbury. It is thought that soldiers killed in the battle were buried at the Austin Friary (a site now occupied by the Sixth Form College) close to Victoria Avenue alongside the River Severn, not far from the Welsh Bridge and splendid half-timbered Rowley's House Museum. Developments and excavations at the friary site in 1910 and 1984 revealed several burials, suggesting a monastic cemetery. Towards the end of the street named Mardol is the mainly 15th century King's Head pub. According to local records, Shakespeare's players performed at the arcaded Market Hall in Market Square, built between 1595 and 1596. The ground floor was once used as a corn market whilst the upper room was occupied by local drapers who bought woolen cloth from North Wales and sold it to people in the clothing industry. Over the open arcades can be seen a figure of Richard, Duke of York, and the arms of Elizabeth 1. In front of the building is a statue of Lord Clive of India, a native of the town.

The town centre is situated within a large meander of the River

Severn – it is almost an island and was easily defensible – but the river is often swollen by rain from the Welsh mountains, which floods the lower parts of the town. It may once have been a Welsh tribal capital, occupied by Saxons, and by 1066 had five churches. After the invasion it was occupied by Roger de Montgomery, the second richest and most powerful Norman after William I, who built a castle. The town and castle underwent further fortification until the Welsh were finally defeated, after which Shrewsbury became a market town. It has many fine buildings, ancient streets and passages, including the quirkily-named 'Grope Lane'. The *Brother Cadfael* novels of Ellis Peters – about a medieval sleuth – are set in and around the splendid sandstone Shrewsbury Abbey, built during the 12th century.

Oxford
Tel: 01865 726871 – TIC

Oxford received six visits from the King's Men during the period 1603–13. A regular calling place for travellers from the Midlands was formerly the Crown Tavern (mentioned in Chapter 6), where Will had a long-standing friendship with the landlord, John Davenant, and his wife. Will stayed there every year when he was travelling between London and Stratford. (He was also godfather to their son William, who was baptised in the nearby St Martin's Parish Church in 1606. According to the gossip at the time, Shakespeare may well have been his natural father).

The tavern was leased by Davenant between 1592 and 1614. (His son William also became a playwright and poet: he introduced scenery on to the stage for his plays, and tried his hand at opera). Behind a facade on the 2nd floor of the former Crown Hotel is the Painted Room, so-named for the well-preserved wall paintings of 1560–80, depicting fruit and flowers. This décor was rediscovered and restored in 1927. Next door is the former coaching inn of the Cross, now the Golden Cross Inn. It stands in a courtyard where the King's Men performed, as they did at a similar courtyard of the King's Head tavern. They also played at the Town Hall and actors were given overnight accommodation in nearby Cornmarket Street. Varying types of entertainment were presented in Oxford during the university's Act and Assize week, which heralded the end of the academic year.

Another Shakespearean link is through the *First Folio* of his works, which the Bodleian Library acquired. Later, it was sold and replaced by a third edition. It was not until 1905, when a *First Folio* was sent to the Bodleian for repair, that it was recognised as the original and was acquired for the Library by public subscription.

Oxford has, for centuries, been famous as a seat of learning, and for the scholarly atmosphere of its magnificent university buildings. The colleges, with their high walls hiding peaceful courtyards and gardens, and the various traditions unique to student life, are intrinsic parts of Oxford's charm. Many famous prime ministers, men of the cloth, the great and the good, have passed through its portals. The number of ancient buildings in the city is boundless – from the architectural splendour of the Radcliffe Camera to the serenity of Christ Church Cathedral, the smallest in England and the only one which is part of a university complex.

From Oxford, the King's Players may have made their way via Bristol or Bath into the West Country, another popular area in their tour schedules.

Bath

Tel: 01225 477101 – TIC

Famous since ancient times for its thermal baths and hot springs, the Romans built the town of Aquae Sulis in the first twenty years after their invasion of Britain in 43AD. The Roman baths and adjacent temple are, in fact, amongst the finest Roman remains in Britain. In medieval times, the springs were Crown property, administered by the church. However, the city was transformed into a fashionable spa in the 18th century, mainly presided over by Regency dandy, Beau Nash. Nearby Bath Abbey is an excellent example of Perpendicular Gothic style. Its construction was begun in 1499, and it has an unusually decorated west front and fine fan vaulting. The city has much Georgian architecture, including Queen Square and the Circus, the Assembly Rooms, and Royal Crescent – designed by John Wood the younger. In Shakespeare's day, the King's Men would probably have performed at the old Guildhall, which continued in use until the 1620s, when it was converted into a shambles for the sale of meat. It was later demolished.

Barnstaple

Tel: 01271 375000

Two visits to the West Country were made by the King's Men in 1605 and 1607, when they acted beside the River Taw at Barnstaple (B1), a major port dealing in shipbuilding and imported textiles from the Continent. The famous stone Long Bridge of sixteen arches spanning the river was built three centuries prior to Shakespeare's birth. In general, players and musicians were welcomed in the town.

By tradition, Barnstaple was granted a charter by King Athelstan in 903AD, making it one of the oldest boroughs in Britain. The town was minting its own coins by the end of the 10th century. At its centre is the oddly twisted 17th century timber-and-lead spire of the parish church, and within strolling distance are Butcher's Row and the covered Pannier Market. With the silting-up of the River Taw, the town's importance as a port was reduced. In front of the collonade is the Tome Stone, where trading agreements were once sealed.

Kent

Tel: 01304 205108 – Dover TIC

From London it was an easy journey into Kent. No doubt, the King's Men would have travelled to Dover by the Old Kent Road – through Rochester, Faversham and Canterbury. Shakespeare wrote about this important English port in the fourth act of *King Lear*. The character of Edgar brought the blinded Gloucester to Dover, making him believe he had fallen over the sheerest cliff of all and survived. Shakespeare goes on to describe 'samphire' – an edible green fleshy plant still said to grow there. The part of the coastline referred to has since become known as Shakespeare's Cliff.

The King's Men also played at Folkestone, Hythe and Romney and, in 1605–06, acted in Maidstone (B6), the county town of Kent, situated on the River Medway. It is thought the troupe performed plays for the mayor or bailiff at the Lower Court House. From Saxon times, this was the site of the county assembly, and the first recorded trial in England was held at Penenden Heath, now a recreation ground. Prior to 975 AD, and until the 16th century, the manor of Maidstone was owned by the Archbishop of Canterbury, who built a house there beside the Medway. It was annexed by Henry VIII, and the manor house (former Archbishop's Palace) was later granted to the Master of the Jewels. Next to the palace is the Church of All Saints, first begun in 1395, which possesses one of the widest naves in England. From the 16th century, various crafts – including weaving – expanded in Maidstone, after Flemish refugees from the Walloon Church settled there to avoid religious persecution.

At the end of the decade, Will went into a form of semi-retirement in Stratford, though he still acted as collaborator with other dramatists. He made occasional trips to London to help supervise production of some of his plays. However, tragedy engulfed the Globe when, during a performance of *Henry VIII* on 29 June 1613, wadding shot from a cannon accidentally set fire to the thatched roof of the theatre. The audience managed to escape without any casualties but the Globe was burned to the ground!

As flies to wanton boys are we to th' gods –
they kill us for their sport

King Lear, Act 4, Scene 1

CHAPTER 9

The Final Years

REBUILDING THE GLOBE was a major priority for the King's Men. It was a miracle that Shakespeare's manuscripts, and those of the other playwrights whose work they performed, were somehow recovered. Costs of rebuilding had to be managed by the housekeepers but it is thought that Will had already relinquished this role in favour of a younger person. He most probably remained a shareholder. The fire also marked his official retirement from the King's Men, and Shakespeare never performed in the re-built theatre.

Will visited London in the spring of 1614, possibly to review the restoration work of the Globe or for the re-opening of the theatre. He was there again in November with his son-in-law, Dr John Hall, to discuss plans regarding his tithe lands at Welcombe and Old Stratford, which he had earlier purchased as joint owner with the town clerk, Thomas Greene. Thereafter, it is thought he finally made New Place in Stratford his permanent home, and it would certainly have given him more time to spend with his wife, family and friends, especially his little grand-daughter, Elizabeth. By 1616, Will's health had begun to fail, and he turned his thoughts to making a will. This he did but, three months later in March, he decided to revise it in order to take account of the changed marital circumstances of his younger daughter, Judith Shakespeare.

The marriage between Judith and Thomas Quiney would not have gone down very well with Shakespeare. The bequests made to his two daughters obviously reflect his displeasure at the actions of his second son-in-law! Will nominated his favourite daughter, Susanna, as virtually sole heir to his fortune, and left minor bequests to many other people.

His wife, Anne, was left his 'second best bed with the furniture (bed hangings)'. The bequest to Anne Shakespeare is rather curious and many have interpreted it as somewhat of a slight upon his wife. However, the bed was an heirloom of the Hathaway family and it was perhaps only right that it should be retained by Anne. Other bequests were to fellow actors Richard Burbage, John Heminges and Henry Condell, to whom he left 26s 8d each, 'to buy them Ringes' (for mourning); to the poor of the parish of Stratford he left £10; and to relatives, friends and neighbours, he bequeathed various personal belongings.

Judith only received a small legacy of £100, a cottage in Chapel Lane, and, providing she or her offspring were surviving three years later, the interest on a further capital sum of £150. Even so, a clause was written into the new will to carefully protect Judith against her husband's wilfulness and extravagence, placing conditions on Thomas Quiney. The couple moved into a house at the corner of Bridge Street and High Street (c4), where Quiney was later convicted for selling unauthorised wines and spirits and allowing drinking on the premises. After some years, he turned his back on his wife, and moved to London. The Stratford property was taken over by relatives, who held it in trust for Judith and her offspring. Today, the building is a retail outlet.

Despite his absence from London, Will's plays continued to form the core of court performances. In May 1613, during the celebrations for Princess Elizabeth's marriage to Frederick v, Elector Palatine of the Rhine, John Heminges produced no fewer than seven of Will's works at Whitehall Palace. Augustine Phillips died in 1605, but Shakespeare's relations with Burbage, Heminges and Condell remained close to the end. James Burbage had died in 1597, but his son Richard made his reputation by creating some of the leading roles in Shakespeare's greatest tragedies – Hamlet, Othello and King Lear were parts in which he always excelled. He and Will were reputedly companions in more than a few 'sporting' activities. One story relates to a time when Burbage was playing Richard iii. He agreed to visit a young woman in the audience after the performance. Shakespeare, overhearing the conversation, anticipated his colleague's action and paid the lady in question an earlier visit himself. On his return, he greeted Richard Burbage with the quip 'William the Conqueror was before Richard the Third!'

According to the testimony of John Ward, the vicar of Stratford, Shakespeare entertained at New Place his two friends, Michael Drayton and Ben Jonson, in the spring of 1616. It seems they 'had a merry meeting,' but drank too hard – for Shakespeare 'died of a fever there contracted.' (A popular local legend, not recorded until 1762, states that as a young man Shakespeare engaged in an intensive drinking bout at nearby Bidford-on-Avon. He and his companions held a convivial drinking contest with local ale drinkers, from which it was said the poet and his friends retired defeated. If true, the site of the contest is thought to have been the Falcon Inn, a large building with origins in the 13th century, situated on the north side of the churchyard in

Bidford. It is a stone house with a west wing, a gabled front of three storeys, and mullioned windows. The building is no longer an inn but a place of private residence, which can be clearly viewed from the exterior in the main street. The village of Bidford stands on the site of an Anglo-Saxon settlement and the parish church of St Laurence dates back to at least 1260.)

It was on 23 April 1616, St George's Day, that Shakespeare died at the age of 52. There is little evidence of the actual circumstances but it may indeed have been caused by excessive drinking and, perhaps, aggravated by a quick attack of pneumonia. Two days later, Will was laid to rest in Holy Trinity Church, Stratford, close to the northern wall of the chancel, in which, as part-owner of the tithes and one of the lay rectors, he had a right to internment. Not far away was the charnel-house, where bones dug up from the churchyard were deposited. This would possibly explain the inscription on Shakespeare's tombstone, thought to have been penned by the Bard himself:

Good friend, for Jesus' sake forbeare
To dig the dust enclosed heare;
Bleste be the man that spares these stones,
And curst be he that moves my bones.

PART TWO

THE WORKS OF WILLIAM SHAKESPEARE

CHAPTER 10

Shakespeare the Traveller

DURING HIS LIFETIME, William Shakespeare was a regular traveller, not just on his journeys between Stratford and London but during the many years he spent on tour with various acting troupes – Lord Leicester's Men, the Lord Chamberlain's Men, the King's Men, and possibly others. There is no concrete evidence that he ever ventured abroad but the fact that he set his plays not only in English locations but in such exotic places as Italy, Greece and Egypt, allows one to speculate upon this possibility. However, an important factor to bear in mind is that many of his plays were adaptations of existing ones by other authors, some of which had already been given a foreign setting. Naturally, *Macbeth* is set in Scotland, *Hamlet* is in Denmark and *Measure for Measure* is given an Austrian backdrop, whilst English historical plays are set at royal palaces, castles, battle fields and sites across Britain, from Northumbria to Kent and the south coast. Some move across the English Channel to France, such as *Henry V*. Other sites stretch from the coast of Wales and on through the Midlands to the Wash, on the east coast. Numerous other plays are based on Roman and Greek historical subjects, and feature a range of locations from Alexandria to Rome and Philippi, Ephesus, and Troy. *A Midsummer Night's Dream* and *Timon of Athens* are both based in Athens while *All's Well That Ends Well* is set in the south of France. *As You Like It* is further north in the Ardennes. *Much Ado About Nothing* takes place in Sicily and *Love's Labour's Lost* in the Navarre. Italy is the location for a number of plays – Venice for *The Merchant of Venice* and *Othello;* Rome for *Julius Caesar* and *Coriolanus;* whilst *Romeo and Juliet* is set in Verona, *Two Gentlemen of Verona* in Milan, and *The Taming of the Shrew* is mainly located in Padua. *The Winter's Tale* depicts Sicily and Bohemia and *Othello* is in Cyprus. The backdrop for *The Tempest* is described as a Mediterranean island, somewhere between Naples and Tunis, whereas the setting for *Twelfth Night* is Illyria, situated on the Dalmatian coast.

So how far did Shakespeare actually travel in order that he had such a commanding knowledge of so many locations at home and abroad? And in what circumstances? It is unlikely we shall ever know the answers, which must lead us to speculation. Perhaps he spent some time as a soldier, which might have provided opportunities for travel on various overseas missions. Or maybe he was a sailor.

To what extent did his travels as an actor take him to distant shores? Certainly some English companies did perform in Scotland and on the Continent. The Queen's Men did a European tour in 1586, including a performance in front of the King of Denmark and the Duke of Saxony. Did this trip take Shakespeare to Elsinore? Was he, perhaps, invited to travel abroad as a guest of one of his sponsors, such as Lord Southampton? Alternatively, given Will met and fraternised with a wide range of people from seamen to aristocrats – even royalty – maybe he gleaned the necessary knowledge from such contacts, including some from overseas. Of course he could well have been delving into the history books of the time. Certainly he gleaned much of his background information for *Macbeth* from the English writer Holinshead's manuscript. He, in turn, had copied his own works from earlier writers, not always separating fact from fiction.

There are so many locations depicted in Shakespeare's works that we can only take a brief look at some of the better-known sites, especially those which can be visited by the tourist, where it still might be possible to discover something of the flavour of the places Shakespeare wrote about. Although far from being a full appraisal of all his works, the author has compiled a selection of plays and sites – some well known, others not so (Chapter 12). These are mainly based in Britain – a brief description of historical background, location and other places of interest which relate to the subject, are included. These are set either under the heading of specific countries or English counties to provide ease of reference for the visitor or Shakespeare enthusiast.

Life is as tedious as a twice-told tale
Vexing the dull ear of a drowsy man

King John, Act 3, Scene 4

CHAPTER 11

Shakespearean Renaissance and Legacy

AFTER SHAKESPEARE'S DEATH, two of Will's most loyal actor colleagues from the King's Men – John Heminges and Henry Condell – spent over seven years compiling into one volume the various manuscripts, texts and notes attributed to their friend's hand. They painstakingly trawled their way through his works checking and re-editing all they could identify – and finally published the *First Folio*. The original publication was entitled *Mr William Shakespeare's Comedies, Histories and Tragedies*. It was published by Edward Blount and Isaac Jaggard and was entered into the Stationers' Register on 8 November 1623. It catalogued thirty-five of Shakespeare's plays (not including *Troilus and Cressida, Pericles, Edward III* or the two narrative poems, 'Venus and Adonis' and 'The Rape of Lucrece') and listed leading actors who played in them. The two compilers, Heminges and Condell, dedicated the publication to that great patron of the arts, William Herbert, 3rd Earl of Pembroke, and to his younger brother, Philip, 1st Earl of Montgomery. With an eye on the future, they also made mention in the dedication of 'any other potential patrons interested in supporting the theatre.' Shakespeare's works continued to be presented in London and by touring companies throughout the country. However, during the Civil War, public performances were banned by Parliamentarians and many theatres were closed or dismantled.

Stratford-upon-Avon and its association with the Bard remained more or less unknown to all but the locals and a few of Shakespeare's London associates for at least a hundred years. There was a lapse in productions and, for some years, little was heard of Shakespeare, apart from in 1675 when he was included in a published list of writers and poets. He was described as 'the glory of the English stage, whose birth at Stratford-upon-Avon is the highest honour that town can boast of.' According to records, the first performance of a Shakespearean play in Stratford was at the Town Hall (c6) in 1746, when *Othello* was staged. Proceeds from this went toward the cost of restoring Will's memorial bust in Holy Trinity Church. Yet, despite his popularity, Stratford was somewhat slow in developing as a centre for visitors. It was in 1769 that the great actor and theatre manager, David Garrick, having been asked to present a statue of the Bard to Stratford's newly-built town hall, decided to stage a Jubilee festival in Shakespeare's honour. He organised teams of tradesmen, costumiers and scene painters from his Drury Lane theatre in London to travel to Stratford. Their task was to erect a wooden amphitheatre in an open space beside the River Avon, possibly somewhere around the site of the present Royal Shakespeare Theatre (C14). Musicians were commissioned to play at the presentations.

The programme for the three-day festival included public processions through the streets, public breakfasts at the Town Hall, horse-racing at Shottery Meadow, the rendering of an oratorio in Holy Trinity Church and a masked ball at the Amphitheatre. The climax of the festival was the recital of a long ode to Shakespeare, orated by no less a person than David Garrick, with music provided by his own orchestra. Unfortunately, the severe weather hampered any outdoor events, and the last day was a washout. Audiences felt let down. However, back in London Garrick recreated on stage what he had intended for Stratford. Strangely, none of Shakespeare's works were presented during the festival. But it did, in a small way, help establish Stratford as a place of literary pilgrimage.

During the latter half of the 18th century, touring groups of players – including that of Roger Kemble – performed plays in Stratford, in a converted barn at the Unicorn Inn in Wood Street and also at the Woolsack Inn, 12-14 Bridge Street. The Shakespeare Club was founded in 1824. Three years later, not only had this body obtained the patronage of King George IV, but a foundation stone was laid for Stratford's first Shakespearean theatre in Chapel Lane – close to the site of the Union Club. This was the Royal Shakespearean Theatre. A festival was held from 23 to 27 April 1830, at which the renowned actor Charles Kean, son of Edmund Kean, performed. Other events were presented in a specially-constructed rotunda building in the Rother Market area.

It was not until 1864, the tercentenary year of the Bard's birth, that a further festival of Shakespearean plays took place in a temporary theatre situated in Southern Lane. Attendance figures for the town were again boosted and, as more and more visitors began to arrive, there was a growing demand for hotel accommodation. Stratford slowly began to realise both the financial and cultural benefits of entertaining visitors. As a result, roads around the town were improved, making it more accessible for horse-drawn vehicles. However, perhaps the most significant development was the introduction of the railway into Stratford, further enhancing the visitor trade.

Royal Shakespeare Theatre, Stratford-upon-Avon

Tel: 01789 403403 – Box Office Tel: 0870 609 1110

Royal Shakespeare Theatre

Prior to the Shakespeare tercentenary celebrations of 1864, discussions took place in both Stratford and London as to how a suitable memorial should be created to commemorate Will's birth. Mr Edward Flower, founder of Stratford's brewery and local benefactor, was a driving force and, along with members of his own family, helped organise and finance the events, which took place in a large wooden pavilion erected in Southern Lane. Unfortunately, the festival was a financial disaster, which led to the pavilion being dismantled and sold. Other ideas were put forward for a memorial and time dragged on. The idea of a permanent memorial was masterminded by Edward's son, Charles Edward Flower, and in 1874 a new theatre was mooted. Charles purchased a piece of land between Waterside and the Clopton Bridge and presented it to the local council as a possible site for the new building.

After discussions with the local authority, the proposal was accepted and the first minutes of the Shakespeare Memorial Association were recorded on 3 March 1875. The aim of this body was to build a theatre and picture gallery, with music room and library wing, and to create a garden to the south of the complex – all in honour of William Shakespeare! The new theatre would be visible from all sides as it stood on the banks of the Avon, and would be fronted by an ornamental pool converted from one of the old canal basins of the Bancroft meadow (this was eventually drained in 1901). A competition was duly launched to find the best design, and public opinion was also taken into consideration. Meetings were held both at the Pump Rooms in nearby Royal Leamington Spa (D14) and at the Town Hall in

Stratford, and submissions whittled down to five finalists. The final choice was made in consultation with Sir Charles Barry, Professor of Architecture at the Royal Academy. The winner was a Gothic building by architects Dodgshun and Unsworth, who were awarded the prize of 25 guineas in July 1876.

The first stage of building comprised the auditorium, stage and dressings rooms; the second included the Shakespeare Memorial Library and Art Gallery wing. The library was housed in two ground floor rooms, with a York stone staircase leading to a saloon. Of interest on the stairs are a group of lancet windows of stained glass, depicting Shakespeare's *Seven Ages of Man*. There are pictorial representations of themes from Shakespeare's works throughout the building.

The Shakespeare Memorial Theatre was officially opened on 23 April 1879 with a performance of *Much Ado About Nothing*. It was the start of the 'Shakespeare Festival', which has since become an annual event. However, the final stage of construction was the erection of the tower in 1883. This contained offices and an area for water storage.

The Memorial Gardens were laid out to the south of the complex alongside the river bank. They had the Shakespeare Monument as a centerpiece, presented by its designer, Lord Ronald Sutherland Gower. The unveiling ceremony for the monument took place on 10 October 1888. Shakespeare and four of his principal characters (Hamlet, Lady Macbeth, Falstaff and Prince Hal) are represented in bronze. The seated figure of the Bard is graceful and gives a hint of an expression of thoughtful intensity. (This monument was removed from the Memorial Gardens in 1933 to its present site in the Bancroft Gardens (C15), overlooking the Clopton Bridge and present tourist information centre (C16). The official opening of Bancroft Gardens was held on Queen Victoria's Golden Jubilee Day, 21 June 1887.

Sadly, during the afternoon of 6 March 1926, smoke was spotted at the Shakespeare Memorial Theatre and by the evening it was a burnt-out shell. Only the library and art gallery survived the disaster.

Temporary theatre accommodation was found at the Stratford Picture House in Greenhill Street, allowing the 1926 Shakespeare Festival to go ahead. It became the venue for the next few years. Meanwhile, plans were being drawn up to build a new theatre and a wide-reaching appeal was launched. Signatories included George Bernard Shaw, Thomas Hardy, Ramsay Macdonald and Stanley Baldwin. Once again, a competition was organised to select a suitable design. This was won by 29-year old Miss Elizabeth Scott, a great niece of Sir Gilbert Scott, and cousin of the architect of Liverpool's Anglican cathedral, Sir Giles Scott. After some disagreement, the new theatre was sited on the banks of the Avon, backing onto the original theatre and overlooking the approximate site of the wooden amphitheatre first built for Garrick's 1769 festival.

Money for the theatre project poured in from supporters all over the world, especially from the United States of America (a plaque in the foyer of the theatre commemorates this generosity). The new Shakespeare Memorial Theatre is a remarkable example of brick architecture but, at the outset, was considered rather controversial. The complex was officially opened by the Prince of Wales (later King Edward VIII) on 23 April 1932, the day of the Shakespeare Birthday Celebrations. The afternoon performance was *Henry IV Part I*, followed in the evening by *Henry IV Part II*. The building was re-named the Royal Shakespeare Theatre in 1961. It takes on a different dimension at night, when all the lights from the balconies, dressing rooms, foyers, bars and restaurant are reflected in the sparkling Avon.

The Royal Shakespeare Company was founded in the same year and, as well as performing in Stratford, the company acted at the Arts Centre and Aldwych Theatre, both in London. In 1986, the RSC was given a permanent London base at the Barbican Arts Centre. Back in Stratford, the original Memorial Theatre was re-developed to create the Swan Theatre. This modern auditorium, echoing the Elizabethan theatre in form, was built within the shell of the old building. At the Swan there is always a nice intimacy between the players and their audiences. (The RSC Collection of paintings and memorabilia is housed in the same building.)

With the main theatre and the Swan operating so close together, there was a need for more rehearsal space and so a large corrugated studio theatre – made of aluminium – was erected in the Paddock, Southern Lane. The building fulfilled various functions for some years and became known as The Other Place (C13). In August 1991 it was rebuilt in local red brick, providing a third permanent auditorium within a short walking distance of the others.

Regular tours of the main theatre complex, backstage areas, dressing rooms, archive, and displays of theatre costumes – worn by famous actors – are regularly organised, but prior booking through the Royal Shakespeare Theatre is necessary.

The Future of Stratford Theatres

At the time of writing, much debate has been taking place as to whether the present main theatre should be demolished and re-built in a more modern style. Thankfully, opinion seems to have come down on the side of retaining what exists but making interior adaptations, such as building an apron stage to suit the requirements of an ever-changing theatre world.

A new theatre complex is being planned on the banks of the Avon, and is due to open in 2009. It will not involve the demolition of any existing building, and is to accommodate 1,000 people. During the interim period, the RSC has received planning permission to erect a building made of Corten steel sheets – already dubbed 'the tin shed' – which will create a sound-proof auditorium to meet high acoustic standards. This will be adjacent to The Other Place and is to be named the Courtyard Theatre. The aim is to reflect the intimacy of the court-yard theatres for which Shakespeare wrote. The Courtyard Theatre is due to open in April 2006.

The architectural brief includes the preservation and restoration of key elements of the 1932 building, including the art deco facade, the foyers and the fountain staircase which links the stalls and circle bars. The Victorian Gothic exterior of the 1879 building – partially destroyed by the 1926 fire – will also be preserved. Front of house facilities will be improved and the existing auditorium will be replaced to provide a modern theatre perspective. The Swan and The Other Place will be retained and a new dedicated space for the Company's educational activity will be created.

The Shakespeare Institute
Tel: 01789 293138

A Shakespeare Institute (C10), which specialises in the study of works by Shakespeare and his contemporaries, was founded in Stratford in 1951 as a graduate centre of the University of Birmingham. It is housed in a building called Mason Croft, the former home of Victorian novelist Marie Corelli. It stands on Church Street, close to the District Council Offices, and holds extensive collections of books and other research material.

Shakespeare Centre
Tel: 01789 201806 / 201836;
Birthplace Trust Records Office – Tel: 01789 201816 / 204016

In 1964 representatives gathered in Stratford to celebrate the 400th anniversary of the Bard's birth. The main project to mark the occasion was the opening of the new Shakespeare Centre (C1), built by the Birthplace Trustees with donations from many nations. It not only houses the headquarters of the Birthplace Trust but provides facilities for educational and academic work, and holds the town's archives and local studies department.

The Centre contains many volumes of books and documents concerning the life and works of William Shakespeare. The building is located overlooking the garden of the Birthplace and was designed by Laurence Williams. The main entrance lobby is enclosed by a series of glass panels engraved by John Hutton with life-size figures of well-known Shakespearean characters. A bronze full-figure statue of Will by Douglas Wain-Hobson symbolises the influence of Shakespeare around the world and provides a striking focal point as one enters the hall.

Shakespeare Birthday Celebrations
For details: Tel: 0870 160 7930 – Stratford TIC

The tradition of an annual procession through the streets of Stratford to Holy Trinity Church, celebrating Shakespeare's birthday, began in the 1890s. This ceremony includes many unique features. The procession, led by a military band, moves off from Waterside into Bridge Street for the unfurling of flags and banners, then on to Shakespeare's Birthplace in Henley Street. A sprig of rosemary is worn by each of the participants 'for remembrance'. From the Birthplace the Parade moves via Henley Street to High Street and Chapel Street. At that point, boys, girls and staff of King Edward VI Grammar School – Will's old school – lead the procession to Holy Trinity Church for the laying of flowers on Shakespeare's grave. In 1896, a link was formed with the Court of St James when the American Ambassador to Britain was invited to the Celebrations. The event has since remained one of the few engagements for the Diplomatic Corps outside of London and includes many foreign ambassadors and high commissioners. Also in the procession are the town council and people of Stratford – many of whom come along in official robes or dressed as Shakespearean characters – together with representatives of the theatre, literature and academe. It is a very colourful event and attracts huge crowds. The celebrations are rounded off with a dinner and a performance of one of Shakespeare's plays in the main theatre.

Shakespeare's Globe, London
Tel: 020 7902 1400; Box Office Tel: 020 7401 9919

Shakespeare's Globe

This is perhaps the most exciting recent development connected with Shakespeare. It began way back in 1949 when the American actor-director, Sam Wanamaker, visited London and went to Bankside in search of a memorial to Shakespeare's original Globe theatre. He was greatly disappointed when all he discovered was a grime-covered bronze plaque set into a brewery wall. Not much of a memorial for one so great! At that moment, the germ of an idea was planted, though it was not to develop for another twenty years. It was Sam's dream to build a replica of the Globe, as near as possible to the original site. He wanted to create an arts, theatre and educational complex incorporating various visitor facilities, and in 1970 established the Globe Playhouse Trust. He also set up a temporary exhibition on Shakespearean theatre in nearby Bear Gardens.

Two years later, Sam met Theo Crosby, who helped and supported him as architect for the project. An international academic committee was formed to discuss, debate and advise on Wanamaker's idea of following the original design and using authentic construction materials. In 1981 an agreement was reached with Southwark Council for a suitable site, some 100 yards (109m) from the original theatre. A dedication ceremony took place two years later. The Shakespeare Globe Trust was founded.

Work started in 1987 and the first oak foundation post was officially driven in by HRH the Duke of Edinburgh on 16 July 1987. The site was cleared and a further ceremony was held on Shakespeare's birthday the following year, at which Dame Judi Dench operated the earth mover to start the building work. It was 1989 before the new Globe's foundations were finally completed; the same year as some of the remains of the Rose Theatre and a part of the great Globe itself were uncovered. Sadly, Sam Wanamaker, mastermind behind the whole project, died on 18 December 1993, but in the knowledge that his dream would be fulfilled. Theo Crosby was to follow him a year later.

The filling-out of the wooden framework of the theatre's walls was the largest lime plastering project in the UK, and the Globe was the first building in the metropolis allowed a thatched roof since the Great Fire in 1666. Despite donations and many fund-raising projects, money was running out. Fortunately, a grant of £12.4 million was awarded from the National Lottery fund in October 1995. By spring 1997, Shakespeare's Globe was completed and ready for its grand opening season, beginning on 8 June with a two-week Festival. Her Majesty the Queen and HRH the Duke of Edinburgh attended a specially-commissioned masque, *Triumphes and Mirth,* on 12 June to celebrate the opening. Sam Wanamaker's daughter Zoë took centre stage to recite the lines from the Prologue to *Henry V.*

As well as the auditorium, galleries, and a sumptuous canopy above the stage, the complex includes the excellent Shakespeare's Globe Exhibition in the basement area. This depicts Shakespeare's life in both Stratford and London, the world of Elizabethan and Jacobean theatre, and the work done in re-building the Globe. The building also has educational facilities for workshops, lectures and courses, sales and souvenir shops, and restaurant and refreshment facilities. The theatre's season runs from May to September, with tours operated throughout the year. It is something of which everyone involved can be justifiably proud. It's certain that Will himself would have approved of this bold new addition to the London skyline.

Nothing emboldens sin so much as mercy

Timon of Athens, Act 3, Scene 5

Other Shakespearean sites in London worth a visit include the splendid statue by Peter Scheemakers in Poets Corner of Westminster Abbey; the reclining effigy of Will in Southwark Cathedral; the dominant statue of the Bard which stands in the centre of Leicester Square Gardens (A11); and – a few miles to the west – David Garrick's Temple to

Shakespeare, designed to house a statue of the Bard by Roubiliac. Set in an 18th century pleasure garden, the temple also contains an exhibition celebrating Garrick's career and life at Hampton. The building was restored in 1999 and is situated on the northern bank of the Thames, close to Hampton Court Palace (temple open Sundays during summer months).

William Shakespeare is the greatest dramatist and poet that England has ever produced and his works have stood the test of time, nearly four hundred years after his death. With a worldwide reputation, he has been translated into many foreign languages. His eye for detail and understanding of the human condition gave him the skills to create characters that seem larger than life. His imaginative lines have introduced many new words, sayings and colloquialisms into the English language. Shakespeare's works include comedies, histories and tragedies, encompassing the whole range of human emotion and experience across the spectrum of his 40 plays, 160 sonnets and narrative poems.

He was born of Warwickshire stock and took much of his early environmental experience with him when he made his way to London and success. Over the years his works have been presented in the theatre and the open air, adapted into musical shows, made into movies and used as blueprints for many other kinds of presentations. Critics, writers and students theorise about the different levels of meaning that Shakespeare included within his works, and often discover a new angle or relevance in today's world. Perhaps his fellow actor-manager and dramatist Ben Jonson best encapsulated the Bard's life and achievements in a line of a memorial poem included in the *First Folio*:

He was not of an age, but for all time.

CHAPTER 12

Play Locations and Other Sites

MOST OF SHAKESPEARE'S works are depicted at specific buildings or sites in Britain, some in countries overseas, and a few in mythical settings. In order to give the reader or tourist a further insight into some of these places, a listing and brief description of the background to each associated site are included. In some cases, reference is also made to the play in which the site appears or to its historical background. Only identifiable sites which can be viewed by the general public, either within or from the exterior, are included and, where possible, a contact telephone number is given.

England

Greater London

Many scenes in Shakespeare's plays and court performances presented to royalty and their guests took place in great royal palaces, both in and around London. It is therefore pertinent to include an initial listing and description of these sites, some of which featured prominently in Shakespeare's life. Many scenes in the plays are set at a Crown property but, in many cases, Will fails to specify exactly which one. Description is often as vague as 'the King's Palace'. The Tower of London is named as the location for scenes in *Henry VI, Part II*, Act 4; *Henry VI, Part III*, Acts 4 & 5; and *Richard III*. However, in the play *Henry VIII*, one might comfortably assume 'the King's Palace' referred to is that of Whitehall.

Royal Palaces and Related Sites

Whitehall Palace – Banqueting House, Whitehall, London SW1A 2ER (A13) Tel: 020 7930 4179

The palace, built by Henry VIII, was the site of the largest complex of royal and government buildings in Britain. It stretched from the present Downing Street to the area of Trafalgar Square and was rather like what might be described as 'a royal village'. The complex also included an area for entertainment and leisure and included tennis courts and bowling alleys.

A main central feature was the Holbein Tower which was retained by the Stuarts during re-building. The Banqueting House was revamped during the reign of James I and included Italian influences and tapestries, some of which are still in service at Hampton Court Palace. However, most of the Whitehall Palace complex was gutted by fire in 1698, after which the royal family moved elsewhere. This took place during the reign of James II – the last monarch to rule with absolute power. Only the Banqueting Hall in Whitehall has survived from the original, together with a section of Tudor brick wall and oriel windows which have been incorporated into the side of the Cabinet Office, but which are only visible from Downing Street. (Some items of furniture were rescued from the original palace and can be seen at Knole *(NT)* (B5), a large stately mansion to the east of Sevenoaks in Kent. This is considered one of England's great treasure houses (a Whitehall infantry stamp was identified underneath the base of some of its chairs).) Access to the Banqueting House in London is daily except Sundays and special occasions. It features a spectacular ceiling by Rubens, comprising of nine massive canvasses. The building was also the site of the execution of Charles I in 1649.

Westminster Abbey, Parliament Square, London SW1P 3PA (A14)
Tel: 020 7222 5152

Henry VI, Part I, Act 1, Scene 1 & Henry IV, Part II, Act 4, Scene 3

The abbey appears in *Henry VI, Part II* as the setting for the funeral of Henry V, when the Dukes of Gloucester, Bedford and other lords are lamenting the young king's recent death as news arrives that English forces have been defeated in France. The Jerusalem Chamber in the abbey is also depicted in *Henry IV, Part II* when King Henry IV dies.

Westminster Abbey is one of the most famous and widely visited of churches in Christendom, originally built as part of a Benedictine monastery by King Edward the Confessor and consecrated in 1065. In the mid-13th century, his successor, Henry III, built flying buttresses and loftier roofs and completed the rebuilding of the old Norman abbey, east of the present choir screen. The nave was constructed throughout the Middle Ages in the same basic style. The Henry VII Chapel, erected in the 16th century, is one of the abbey's greatest glories.

The connection with monarchy has been maintained down the

years in various ways. It is the scene of coronations as well as the place of burial of many earlier kings and queens of England (including Elizabeth I and her arch-rival, Mary Queen of Scots). George II was the last monarch to be interred within its walls. Elizabeth I converted the monastery into the Collegiate Church of St Peter in Westminster, entrusting its direction to a Dean and Chapter. Members of the monarchy, churchmen, prominent statesmen, musicians and military, literary and professional people are either buried or memorialised in the abbey. A favourite area is that known as Poets' Corner in the South Transept and includes a fine statue of Shakespeare by Peter Scheemakers – placed there in 1740 – as well as tributes to Chaucer, Shelley, Byron, Dickens, Noel Coward and many others from the field of the arts.

Westminster Hall, Parliament Square, London SW1 1AA (A14)
Tel: 020 7219 4272

Richard II, Act 4, Scene 1

Westminster Hall (A14) is the setting when Bolingbroke summons Richard II to confirm his abdication. Though the King still feels he rules by divine right, he invites Bolingbroke to grab the crown. He, in turn, orders Richard to the Tower of London.

The Hall, first built by William Rufus in 1099, is the only part of the medieval palace of Westminster which remains. From the 13th to 19th centuries, it was used as the country's highest court of law and witnessed the trials of Thomas More, Guy Fawkes and Charles I. Oliver Cromwell was proclaimed Lord Protector here in 1653, but, after the Restoration, his head was displayed on a spike above the entrance. Today, it is the scene of lying-in-state for prominent members of the royal family and, very occasionally, great statesmen. Regular tours of the Palace of Westminster include an opportunity to see inside this historic building.

St James's Palace, Cleveland Row, Marlborough Gate, London SW1 (A12)

The palace (A12) was built between 1532-40 by Henry VIII, on the site of a former lepers' hospital. St James's and Whitehall Palaces originally formed part of the Palace of Westminster. The main red-brick turreted gate-tower on the north front which looks onto St James's Street is the most conspicuous reminder of Tudor days and stands beside the Chapel Royal, leading into Colour Court, the former Great Court. It is known as the senior palace of the Sovereign and was occupied by kings and queens for over 300 years. Elizabeth I was resident there during the campaign against the Spanish Armada and set out from St James's to address her troops assembled at Tilbury. Charles I spent the night at St James's, prior to his execution in January 1649, in order to avoid hearing his scaffold being erected in Whitehall. Only a few original features remain of the south front, where royal apartments are built around Friary Court with gates which open into St James's Park. The existing State Rooms overlooking The Mall have a Tudor-style exterior. Two rooms at the west end were added by Sir Christopher Wren for James II and used as the Great Drawing Room and Council Chamber. When most of Whitehall Palace burned down in 1698, St James's became the principal royal residence.

The south and east ranges of Friary Court were also destroyed by fire in 1809 and today Marlborough Road bisects the site, dividing the Queen's Chapel from the remainder of the palace. This chapel was designed by Inigo Jones for use by Queen Henrietta Maria, the Roman Catholic Consort of Charles I. Today, the site houses various members of the royal family and their respective offices, the Lord Chamberlain, and the Ambassador to the Court of St James. Unfortunately, there is no public access to the palace with the exception of the Chapel Royal, which is open for special services along with the Queen's Chapel in Friary Court, where Handel composed some of his more famous works. Nearby is Clarence House, home of Charles, Prince of Wales, and the Duchess of Cornwall.

The Tower of London, London EC3 4AB (A7)
Tel: 0870 756 6060

Henry VI, Part I, Acts 1 & 2; Henry VI, Part II, Act 4; Henry VI, Part III, Acts 4 & 5 & Richard III, Acts 1 and 4.

The Tower of London is the setting for four of Shakespeare's plays. It was built by William the Conqueror as a simple watchtower but by 1100 had evolved into both fortress and palace. The inner curtain wall, with its numerous towers, was built at the time of Henry III and added to by Edward I. The first king to be imprisoned there was Richard II but he was later freed. Other famous prisoners include Sir Thomas More, Queens Anne Boleyn and Catherine Howard, Lady Jane Grey, Elizabeth Tudor – later to become Elizabeth I – the Earls of Essex and Strafford, and Sir Walter Raleigh. Most of them were executed. It was in the Tower that the two princes were kept before they disappeared without trace – the murderer was thought to have been Richard III, though in Shakespeare's play Richard hires James Tyrell to complete the job on his behalf.

Shakespeare's friend and sponsor, the Earl of Southampton, was also confined to the Tower in 1601 for his part in the abortive Essex Rebellion. Today, the complex is a barracks, armoury and museum. In 1994 the crown jewels, traditionally kept in a bunker in the keep (the White Tower), were moved to a specially designed showcase – the Jewel House – situated above ground level. This tower also houses armoury displays, including original armour worn by Henry VIII and Charles I.

Greenwich Palace, Greenwich, London SE3 (B9)
Tel: 0870 608 2000 – Greenwich TIC

Greenwich was the most easterly of the palaces built beside the Thames. In 1417, the manor passed to Humphrey, Duke of Gloucester, who built the palace ten years later. In 1433, two hundred acres were enclosed as part of the royal estate which was re-named Placentia – a rambling complex which has disappeared.

Important visitors arriving by sea were received by various monarchs at Greenwich and the manor and palace were enlarged by Henry VII. His son, the future Henry VIII, was born there on 28 June 1491 and baptised by the Bishop of Exeter at the local St Alfege's Church, since rebuilt. The younger Henry preferred Greenwich to nearby Eltham Palace as a place of residence and his marriage to Catherine of Aragon took place at Greyfriars Church, Greenwich, in 1511. Both his elder daughter, Mary Tudor (from his first marriage) and his younger daughter, Elizabeth Tudor (from his marriage to Anne Boleyn) were born at Greenwich, in 1516 and 1533 respectively. Edward VI, Henry's son and heir from the marriage to Jane Seymour, died there on 6 July 1553 at the age of 16. During her reign, Elizabeth I made various alterations to the palace, which became her main place of residence. It was at Greenwich Palace that, by tradition, Sir Walter Raleigh threw down his cloak to protect the Queen from stepping into a puddle.

Elizabeth enjoyed sailing on the Thames and from her base at Greenwich visited the royal shipyards at Woolwich and Deptford, where *The Golden Hinde* was later laid up as a national memorial to the circumnavigation of the world by Sir Francis Drake. On his accession,

James I erected a brick frontage to the palace and his Queen, Anne of Denmark, laid the foundation stone of Queen's House near to the Park. Their daughter, Princess Mary, was baptised at Greenwich in 1606. After the reigns of later monarchs Charles I and Charles II, who preferred Hampton Court and Kensington palaces, the old palace at Greenwich was incorporated into the new Naval Hospital (closed 1869). Four years later, it became the Royal Naval College, a majestic Baroque ensemble which opens onto the Thames and perfectly frames the Queen's House beyond. The college includes the magnificent Painted Hall, dominated by James Thornhill's exquisite ceiling paintings. The National Maritime Museum occupies the west wing of the former Naval Asylum on Romney Road.

Richmond Palace, Richmond, Surrey TW9 (B10)
Tel: 0208 940 9125

The palace, built in the 12th century, first known as Sheen Palace, was acquired by Henry I in 1125. The first king to frequent the place was Edward III, who died there in 1377. Richard II demolished the property after his Queen, Anne of Bohemia, died there of the plague. Henry V restored it and Edward IV held jousting tournaments on the green. Henry VII was fond of Sheen, though it was burnt down early in his reign. He rebuilt the property and changed its name to Richmond Palace, after his own Yorkshire earldom. At the same time, he built a new edifice, leaded windows and a tower. His son, Henry VIII, later granted the place to his fourth wife, Anne of Cleves, as part of their divorce settlement. Queen Mary Tudor and Philip of Spain spent part of their honeymoon at Richmond. Her sister, Elizabeth I, regularly used the palace and the Lord Chamberlain's Men, later the King's Men, often performed there. It was at Richmond Palace that Elizabeth died on a bed of cushions on 23 March 1603.

Her successor, James I, moved his court to Richmond on a regular basis and invited Shakespeare's players to perform for him. During the Commonwealth the old palace fell into disuse and it was demolished in the 18th century. The old deer park to the north was both garden and park and, bordering the river, contains Sir William Chambers' Observatory, completed 1769.

Little remains of Henry VIII's splendid building. Facing Richmond Green is a simple gateway from Henry VII's time, with large and small stone arches, with his coat of arms over the larger. The gateway once led into the outer courtyard of the palace, now named Old Palace Yard. Henry VII died at Richmond on 21 April 1509, aged 52, having ruled England for 24 years. The property has been restored and renovated on many occasions since being placed into private ownership. The nearby Museum of Richmond at the Old Town Hall, Whittaker Avenue, has a detailed model of the palace in its glory days.

Hampton Court Palace, East Molesey, Surrey KT8 9AU (B11)
Tel: 0870 752 7777

The palace began life as an ecclesiastical house, built in 1516 by Cardinal Wolsey, Chancellor to Henry VIII. The site was transformed from an agricultural estate with the addition of new kitchens, lodgings and gardens. However, with Wolsey's failure to bring about a

Hampton Court Palace

papal annulment of Henry's marriage to Catherine of Aragon, Henry dismissed him and seized the palace. It became the King's main home – the only one capable of housing his entire court. All six of his wives stayed at Hampton Court and it was there that Jane Seymour gave birth to the future Edward VI, dying in the process. The scale of the palace necessitated building great kitchens to feed Henry's large court and guests.

During the reigns of Elizabeth I and James I, the palace was renowned for its masques, plays and balls, and during the Civil Wars it was first a refuge, then a prison for Charles I. It was put up for sale but without takers so Cromwell decided to take over the place himself and lived there as Lord Protector until his death in 1658. The only surviving theatre at which Shakespeare's plays were performed during his lifetime is at Hampton Court Palace. Of specific interest is the Great Hall, the Great Watching Chamber, the Actors' Tyring Room, the Horn Room, and the Haunted Gallery. Shakespeare's plays were presented in the Great Hall and the audience would have watched from either side of the stage. The most important guests and courtiers were given reserved seats near to the royal family at the far end of the hall. It is said that sometimes, during performances, hot wax dripped onto the audience from the chandeliers strung across the ceiling on wires.

The gardens at Hampton Court were laid out by Charles II but, during the reign of William III and Mary, Sir Christopher Wren was commissioned to rebuild the palace. He constructed the east and south wings, added the banqueting house and completed the chapel. Due to an unhappy childhood spent at the palace, George III disliked the place, but he established grace-and-favour residences for courtiers in the royal household. Eventually, the palace was opened to the public by Queen Victoria in 1838.

Windsor Castle, Windsor, Berkshire SL4 (B12)
Tel: 020 7766 7304

Henry IV, Parts I & II; Henry VI, Part I

Windsor Castle is featured in all three plays and the castle's Council Chamber is also mentioned in *Henry IV, Part I,* Act 1, Scene 3.

The castle began life in the form of a wooden keep built by William the Conqueror as a stronghold to guard the approaches to London from the west. It is first mentioned in the Domesday Book of 1086 and remained a purely military establishment until 1110 when Henry I moved there from his palace in Old Windsor. His son, Henry II, dismantled the wooden building and rebuilt it in stone in the 13th century. Shortly after his death, the castle suffered its first siege when English barons attacked Prince John's army of Welshmen, who had taken refuge within its walls. The troops took flight whilst John escaped to France. He eventually returned to Windsor as King in 1215 and was forced to sign the Magna Carta at nearby Runnymede.

Elizabeth I loved Windsor and built the North Terrace with its commanding view across the river and Home Park. She also planted a great colony of oaks in Windsor Forest and invited Shakespeare and his players to perform at the castle on many occasions.

With the passing of the Tudor dynasty, the Stuarts took over the throne but Windsor was not favoured by James I. The unhappy Charles I went there as a child in 1603 and was imprisoned in his own apartments shortly before his execution in 1649. He was finally laid to rest in the same vault as Henry VIII and Jane Seymour in St George's Chapel. During the Civil Wars the castle was used by Cromwell as a garrison. It was not until the restoration of Charles II that the royal apartments were remodelled into what are now the State Apartments.

During the reign of George III, monarchy used Windsor on a regular basis. Queen Victoria loved the place and spent much of her long reign there in exile. It has remained a favourite residence of the royal family ever since. In 1992, a disastrous fire broke out in the castle, completely gutting the main banqueting area, St George's Hall. It has since been lovingly restored.

Site of Baynard's Castle, Blackfriars, London EC3 (A9)
Tel: 0870 444 3852 – Museum of London

Richard III, Act 3, Scene 7

Baynard's Castle (A9) is the setting for the scene in which Richard, Duke of Gloucester, is greeted rather hesitantly by local citizens. Though he has no popular support from the people of London, Buckingham still contrives that Richard is offered the crown. The castle was a residence on the north bank of the Thames near Blackfriars. It was founded by Baynard, a nobleman at the time of the Norman Conquest, and owned by the Duke of York, father to Richard III. The original castle was destroyed around 1275 and rebuilt at the nearby riverside area in 1428 as a prominent waterfront town-house. Excavations carried out in 1972 revealed the foundations of the Tudor castle, overlying earlier tenements and the East Watergate, in an area to the east of Blackfriars Bridge, just beyond Puddle Dock. It was extensively modified by Henry VII who refaced the frontage with a series of five projecting towers. The north side of the castle lay on Thames Street and the excavations revealed the entrance and a chamber to the east. However, little remains to be seen by the public.

Site of the Battle of Barnet, Barnet, Greater London EC5 (B13)
Tel: 0208 440 8066 – Barnet Museum; or
Tel: 0208 959 6657 – Barnet Archives

Henry VI, Part III, Act 5, Scenes 2 & 3

Shakespeare depicts two battle scenes at Barnet (B13). The action commences when Edward IV brings in the wounded Richard Neville, Earl of Warwick – sometimes known as 'The Kingmaker' – and flings him down to die. In reality, the battle between the Yorkists and Lancastrians was fought in heavy mist on 14 April 1471. There was a misunderstanding between the armies and all ended in confusion, with troops finding they were fighting men from their own side. The Yorkists under King Edward won the day, dashing the hopes of their opponents, led by Warwick. Warwick was struck down whilst manoeuvring to regain his charger.

Parts of the battlefield remain, preserved in a golf course, common and village green to the west of Moncton Hadley, near Barnet. The triangular Hadley Green, alongside the old Great North Road, (half a mile (1km) north of Barnet), is the place where Warwick fell. The battle is commemorated by an obelisk, erected by Sir Jeremy Sambrooke in 1740, just to the north of the battlefield.

Berkshire

The Merry Wives of Windsor

The whole of Shakespeare's play, first performed in 1602, is set both within and around the town of Windsor. One theory is that it was written for the Ceremony of the Knights of the Garter when Lord Hunsdon, patron of the Lord Chamberlain's Men, was installed in St George's Chapel. The actual play would have been staged in Westminster Palace. There was also a rumour that Queen Elizabeth requested Shakespeare to write about Falstaff, a fictional character from an earlier play, falling in love, but this has not been proven.

Sites include:

Windsor Castle, Windsor, SL4 – See under 'Royal Palaces & Related Sites'

St George's Chapel, Windsor Castle SL4 (B12)
Tel: 020 7766 7304

Edward III was born at Windsor Castle in 1312. In 1346, while he danced at a celebratory function with Joan, the young Countess of Salisbury, one of her garters slipped down and fell upon the ballroom floor. This raised some amusement, causing great embarrassment to the lady. The King rebuked those who laughed, picked up the garter, and assured them he would make it famous throughout history. Later, he announced his fraternity of Knights was to be called the Order of the Garter. In 1472, Edward IV built a grander chapel for the Knights, which became the present St George's Chapel, a fine example of Perpendicular architecture. The chapel has many memorials and is the burial place of every later monarch, excluding Queen Victoria and

Prince Albert – who are buried at the nearby Frogmore Mausoleum – and Edward VIII (later Duke of Windsor), who is buried in the nearby royal burial ground with his wife, the Duchess (the former Mrs Wallis Simpson). George VI and his consort, Elizabeth, the late Queen Mother, are both buried in St George's Chapel.

Harte & Garter Hotel, High Street, Windsor SL4 1PH (B12)
Tel: 01753 863426

The hotel stands in the High Street, opposite the castle. The existing building dates back to the mid-19th century. The site has long been associated with traditional English inns and was once known as the Garter Inn. It is thought to have been frequented by theatrical circles as far back as the 1600s and was the setting for scenes in Shakespeare's *The Merry Wives of Windsor*. However, there is no positive evidence of the existence of a Garter Inn in Windsor, either during the time of Henry V or of Shakespeare. The name in the play is likely to have been suggested by Falstaff's title as 'Knight of the Garter'.

Windsor Great Park, SL4 (B12)
Tel: 01753 743900 – Windsor TIC

This was part of a vast Norman hunting chase set in 5,000 acres of the Surrey and Berkshire countryside, stretching from Windsor Castle in the north to Ascot in the south. The Great Park was enclosed for the hunting of deer and wild boar during the 13th century and its royal connections go back to the time of King Edward the Confessor. At one corner of the Park are some dozen oaks, all as old as the Norman Conquest. Shakespeare memorialises 'Herne's Oak' in *The Merry Wives of Windsor* (it was he who invented the 'Herne the Hunter' legend). The oak generally known as Herne's was blown down in a storm of 1863 and a sapling was planted on the spot. It is however unlikely that Will was writing about any specific tree and its identification most probably came later as a result of the play. Purchases of land by Charles II in 1680 enabled the planting of a great avenue of elm trees, called the Long Walk, leading from the castle to Virginia Water. (There are various access points to the Park and Long Walk via the High Street.)

Cambridgeshire

Kimbolton Castle, Kimbolton, Huntingdon PE28 0EA (E22)
Tel: 01480 860505 – School

Henry VIII, Act 4, Scene 2

Originally a medieval castle, Kimbolton (E22) was the final residence of Catherine of Aragon during her exile after being reduced to the rank of Princess Dowager. Part of Act 4, Scene 2 is set in the castle, which is given the name 'Kimbleton'. It was largely rebuilt in the 18th century as a country house for the Earls and Dukes of Manchester, its owners for nearly 350 years. It is now home to Kimbolton School but retains some outstanding Pellegrine murals and a fine collection of portraits. The building is set in extensive wooded grounds, close to the small town of Kimbolton and open on certain days or by appointment. Kimbolton is on the B645 almost midway between Cambridge and Northampton, with easy access from the A1 trunk road.

Gloucestershire

Tewkesbury GL20 (B20)
Tel: 01684 295027 – Tewkesbury TIC

Henry VI, Part III, Act 5 & Richard II

Immediately after the Battle of Barnet, when the Earl of Warwick was defeated and killed, Queen Margaret and her son arrived back in England at Weymouth. The Lancastrians soon rallied to her cause. The army was put under joint command of Edward, Prince of Wales, and the Duke of Somerset, and was marched north to join with Jasper Tudor in Wales. Edward IV speedily gathered more troops to intercept the Queen and Somerset before they could cross the River Severn at Gloucester. Unfortunately, the duke's contingent was short of additional arms and supplies so had to enter Bristol to acquire re-enforcements. The timing of this was fatal as the Duke of Gloucester (the future Richard III) closed the city's gates to Somerset. On 3 May 1471, he took a decision to fight his ground for the Queen at Tewkesbury (B20), duly placing 6,000 troops ready for attack. On the following day, King Edward bombarded his enemies, forcing Somerset to lead an attack. Somerset's soldiers were forced back as the King's troops advanced to defeat them. Many troops were slaughtered and it was thought that up to 2,000 died in battle. The troublesome Queen Margaret escaped to France but her son Edward, Prince of Wales, was killed. Somerset was arrested at the nearby abbey, where he had taken sanctuary after the battle.

Site of the Battle of Tewkesbury, Tewkesbury GL20 (B20)
Tel: 01684 295027 – Tewkesbury TIC

Henry VI, Part III, Act 5, Scenes 4 & 5 & Richard III

To the south of Tewkesbury Abbey are the fields which in 1471 saw the penultimate and most decisive battle in the Wars of the Roses. Bloody Meadow, near the abbey, was the scene of a ferocious battle. The Lancasterian army, under Somerset, took up positions on Lincoln Green, Gupshill Manor and a site known as Queen Margaret's camp. It was here that Edward IV overpowered Somerset's forces and led the Yorkists to victory. A way-marked route takes visitors from Vineyards car park and around the battle trail, with regular guided walks arranged.

Tewkesbury Abbey, Tewkesbury GL20 5RZ (B20)
Tel: 01684 850959

The abbey was built in the 12th century on the former site of a Benedictine monastery. It has a magnificent Norman tower, which dominates the local skyline. The building is one of the largest abbey churches to survive the Dissolution as the townsfolk managed to redeem it from Henry VIII for £400. There are a number of fine tombs in the church and the glorious Warwick Chantry, endowed by the family of Richard Neville, Earl of Warwick.

Berkeley Castle, Berkeley GL13 9BQ (B22)
Tel: 01453 810332

Richard II, Act 2, Scene 2

It is Berkeley Castle to which Edmund of Langley, Duke of York, refers when he tells loyalists to 'meet me presently'. Rebellious Bolingbroke also marches there. When they meet, York feebly opens the castle to him and from that time on King Richard is doomed. The story of this incident is also recounted by Hotspur in *Henry IV, Part I*, Act 1, Scene 3.

The castle, a compact classic fortress, complete with circular Norman keep and inner bailey, is still the home of the Berkeley family after 900 years. It has two main claims to historical fame. Firstly, it was in the splendid Great Hall that the Barons met in 1215 before proceeding to Runnymede to force the Magna Carta upon King John. Secondly, according to Marlowe's dramatisation *Edward II*, King Edward II was horribly murdered in 1327 in the dungeon of the keep by having a piece of red hot metal inserted into his rear. This is not in fact true and his death was falsified. He most probably died overseas in 1341.

Hampshire

Southampton SO14 7JP (B3)
Tel: 023 8022 1106 – Southampton TIC

Henry V, Act 2, Scene 2 (and Chorus)

King Henry V prepared to sail from Southampton (B3) seeking proof of his right to rule over France. This was to lead to the Battle of Agincourt, where the French army was defeated with heavy losses. In 1415, the King and his troops would have passed through Southampton's Westgate, which led to their departure point, West Quay, the waterfront on the River Test. (It was from the same point that the Pilgrim Fathers made an aborted departure for the New World on 5 August 1620). On the south side of Westgate is the half-timbered Tudor Merchants Hall, which originally stood in St Michael's Square and was used as a woollen cloth hall. Nearby St Michael's Church was founded about 1070. Opposite is the Tudor House, the finest half-timbered house in Southampton, and once the home of a rich merchant.

Herefordshire

Site of the Battle of Mortimer's Cross, nr Leominster HR6 9PD (E20)
Tel: 01432 268430 – Hereford TIC

Henry VI, Part III, Act 2, Scene 1

On 2 February 1461, Edward, Prince of Wales, defeated Jasper Tudor, Earl of Pembroke and uncle to Henry Tudor (the future Henry VII), at the Battle of Mortimer's Cross (E20). This was more of a regional fight between the Welsh and Marcher supporters of York and Lancaster rather than a full-scale battle between two armies. However, after the so-called battle, Edward, Earl of March, beheaded ten knights and esquires from the English border counties. The battle site is located approximately 5 miles (8km) north west of Leominster, close to the junction of the A4100 with the B4362, and is commemorated by a memorial.

Hereford HR4 8BW (B21)
Tel: 01432 268430 – Hereford TIC

Jasper Tudor was executed and his head taken to Hereford (B21) to be displayed on the steps of the High Cross at the west end of Hightown. One hundred candles are said to have been placed around the cross to illumine the gruesome scene. A plaque marking the site can be seen outside Marks and Spencer in the High Street. After several more battles, Edward marched on London, where he was proclaimed Edward IV on 3 March 1461.

Hertfordshire

Site of the Battle of St Albans, St Albans AL3 (B14)
Tel: 01727 864511 – St Albans TIC

Henry VI, Part II, Act 5, Scenes 2 & 3

On 22 May 1455, a battle – perhaps more of a skirmish – took place both within and around the city of St Albans (B14). The Duke of York and his army moved south from Yorkshire to intercept the King, hoping to slay the Duke of Somerset. York had already lined up his allies – including Salisbury and Warwick – along with their armies. Fighting commenced but less than 100 men were slain, including Somerset. Eventually York was restored by the King as Lord Protector. The battle is commemorated by a blue plaque set on the side of a building society in Victoria Street. It specifies that on the same site stood the Castle Inn, before which the Second Duke of Somerset fell.

Cathedral & Abbey Church of St Alban, St Albans AL3 (B14)
Tel: 01727 860780

The present cathedral is reputed to have been built on the site where Alban, a Roman soldier, was executed in AD 209, becoming the first Christian martyr in England. A Benedictine monastery was founded in AD 793 but replaced by the fine Norman building we see today, overlooking the ancient Roman town of Verulamium. The abbey was abandoned at the Dissolution in 1539 and many adjacent monastic buildings were destroyed. In 1553 it was sold to the local townsfolk for use as a parish church but fell into a state of disrepair, bordering on ruin. However, it was lovingly restored in the late 19th century. The abbey boasts the longest nave in the country – at 550 feet – and some wonderful Norman architecture has been retained. A few of the knights who fought in the Battle of St Albans were interred in the abbey, which was elevated to cathedral status in 1877. It is also the last resting place of Lord Robert Runcie, former Bishop of St Albans and latterly Archbishop of Canterbury.

Kent

Shakespeare's Cliff, Dover CT16 (B7)
Tel: 01304 205108 – Dover TIC

King Lear

Scenes in this play are depicted at various points in and around Dover. In particular, Shakespeare's Cliff, west of the town and close to the A20, takes its name from the playwright's reference to the site (though no specific cliff is mentioned in the play). In October 1604, around the time Shakespeare was writing *King Lear*, the King's Men visited Dover to perform. The cliff can be reached by trails which lead from a council estate and up past a recreation ground.

Leicestershire

Bosworth Battlefield (EH), Sutton Cheney, nr Market Bosworth, Nuneaton CV13 0AD (E18)
Tel: 01455 290429

Richard III, Act 5, Scenes 3–7

The Battle of Bosworth (E18) took place on 22 August 1485 and was one of the last battles in the Wars of the Roses, in which Richard III died, defeated by Henry Tudor, Earl of Richmond. The latter was ultimately crowned as Henry VII, the first ruler of the Tudor dynasty. Places of interest include the Battlefield visitor centre; a

King Richard's Well

Battlefield trail – which includes Ambion Hill, where Richard is thought to have raised his standard; King Richard's Well – from which he drank during the battle; and King Richard's Field – where he fell and breathed his last. On his way to battle, Richard and his troops passed the 11th century church of St James, Sutton Cheney. A number of graves in the churchyard of St James the Greater in Dadington contain the remains of soldiers slain during the fighting. Crown Hill at Stoke Golding is where Henry Tudor is supposed to have received the royal crown.

Castle Gardens, Leicester LE1 (E19)
Tel: 0116 299 8888 – Leicester TIC

A bronze statue of Richard III by James Butler was unveiled in 1980. It stands at the gates of Castle Gardens in Leicester city centre (E19) and looks towards Bow Bridge, where Richard's death was predicted in August 1485.

Northumberland

Warkworth Castle & Hermitage (EH), Warkworth, Northumberland NE66 0UJ (F1)
Tel: 01665 711423

Henry IV, Part I, Act 2, Scene 3 & Henry IV, Part II, Act I, Scene I & Act 2, Scene 3

Standing high above the River Coquet, Warkworth Castle (F1) once played a major role in defending Northern England during the border wars of the Middle Ages. There are scenes in the castle in both plays – it was the stronghold of the powerful Percy family, presented to them by Edward III, who thought it a suitable reward for Henry Percy II's help in repelling the marauding Scots. His grandson, Henry Percy IV, was created Earl of Northumberland in 1377 and built the magnificent keep. In *Henry IV, Part II*, Shakespeare has the character Rumour describe it as 'the worm-eaten hold of ragged stone'. In the rebellion which broke out in 1403, the earl's son, also named Henry Percy IV (better known as Hotspur) was killed at the Battle of Shrewsbury. In 1405, having helped depose Richard II, Henry Percy rebelled yet again against Henry IV. When attacked, the family was forced to surrender the castle and it again became Crown property.

Shropshire

Site of the Battle of Shrewsbury, Shrewsbury SY4 3DB (E16)
Tel: 01743 281200 – Shrewsbury TIC

Henry IV, Part I, Act 4, Scenes 1 & 3; Act 5, Scenes 1–5

The backgrounds for these scenes are the royal and the rebel camps near to the town. In Act 5, Scenes 3–5, the setting is the battlefield to the north east of Shrewsbury.

In 1399, Henry Bolingbroke, Duke of Lancaster, seized the throne from Richard II and was duly crowned Henry IV, helped by the powerful Sir Henry Percy, Earl of Northumberland. Feeling inadequately rewarded, the Percys rallied Northern opposition to the King. Under the brilliant command of young Harry Percy (Hotspur), a vast army of 20,000 men marched south to join the charismatic Welsh leader, Owen Glyndwr at Chester (E7). The King arrived at Lichfield, where he discovered that Hotspur was advancing on Shrewsbury. Both Hotspur and Henry arrived on 20 July, the royal army camping on the hill to the south of Haughmond Abbey *(EH,* Tel: 01743 709661). Hotspur's troops were a few miles west, near to the River Severn. A battle took place between the two sides on the following day at a site about 2 miles (3.2km) north of Shrewsbury (E16). There was much fierce fighting but finally the King's son, the future Henry V (Prince Hal), broke the enemy line and attacked from the rear. In the confusion the Percy force was broken, Hotspur was killed and the day was lost. King Henry IV later founded a Battlefield church *(CCT)* on the site of his victory to commemorate those who were slain. It can be visited as part of a Battlefield trail, 3 miles (5km) north east of Shrewsbury, signposted off the A49 (key holder nearby). In Shrewsbury town centre is a plaque on Barclays Bank, at the corner of Castle Street with St Mary's Street, which states that on that site, on Monday 23 July 1403, the dead body of Hotspur was placed between two mill stones and afterwards beheaded and quartered. Also of interest in the town is the Henry Tudor House in Wyle Cop, where Henry Tudor, Earl of Richmond, stayed in August 1485 on his way to Bosworth Field, where he was later to be proclaimed as King Henry VII.

Suffolk

Bury St Edmunds IP33 (E24)
Tel: 01284 764667 – Bury St Edmunds TIC

Henry VI, Part II & King John

Scenes in both plays are set in or around the ancient city of Bury St
Edmunds (E24). In the former drama the abbey is the setting for Act 3,
Scene 1, but much of the property was destroyed or incorporated into
other buildings after the Dissolution. Two gateways remain, including
the very fine abbey gate. The tower, set in the abbey precinct wall, was
once the main entrance to the monastic buildings which now form the
main entrance to abbey gardens. Ruins of the west front of the former
abbey had been converted into houses by the time of the Restoration.
The Norman section, known as Samson's Tower, was opened in 1993
as an exhibition centre to interpret the history of the abbey and its environs. In *Henry VI, Part II*, Act 3, Scene 2, the setting is also in Bury St
Edmunds, in a room at Cardinal Beaufort's house. Of interest is the
nearby cathedral – the only one in Suffolk – and 14th century St Mary's
Church, which has an impressive roof over the nave. Henry VIII's
younger sister, Mary Tudor, was re-interred in the Sanctuary when her
tomb was transferred from the abbey after its demise.

Warwickshire

Warwick Castle, Warwick CV34 4QU (D12)
Tel: 0870 442 2000

Henry VI, Part III, Act 4

Although the scene is titled 'A Plain in Warwickshire', one can assume
it is in the vicinity of the castle, which once belonged to Richard Neville,
Earl of Warwick (The Kingmaker), who lived there between 1449–71.
He was meeting with the Earl of Oxford and welcoming the Dukes of
Clarence and Somerset. The mighty fortress would have been well-
known to Shakespeare. It is set on the River Avon, a few miles above
Stratford. An early Norman castle on the site was destroyed in 1264
and earliest masonry dates from the 14th century Beauchamp recon-
struction. It is dominated by their two great towers, Caesar's and
Guy's, both noted as fine examples of military architecture. Caesar's
Tower is 147 feet high and commands the river crossing with imposing
might. Soon after its completion, it was used to house prisoners taken

during the Battle of Poitiers in 1356 and an unusual feature is a dungeon within a dungeon – known as the 'oubliette'. An unfortunate prisoner had just sufficient room to lie in complete darkness. The towers are connected by an embattled wall enclosing the Inner Court, an area protected from attack by a deep dry moat, a drawbridge and two sturdy portcullises with double doors. The interior of the castle is magnificently furnished, especially the Great Hall, with its displays of armoury, where Piers Gaveston, favourite of Edward II, was tried and found guilty of treason in 1312.

After remaining Crown property for some years the castle was granted in 1547 to John Dudley, Earl of Warwick (1547–53). He became a great power in the land and vied with the Duke of Somerset for the favour of the young King, Edward VI. In 1551 he unseated Somerset and became the King's Chief Minister, but did not hold high office for long as Edward died two years later. It was this John Dudley who, on the death of Edward VI, tried to put Lady Jane Grey, his daughter-in-law, on to the throne of England. Failing in this venture, he was attained in the first Parliament of Queen Mary Tudor and beheaded on Tower Hill in 1553. He left two sons – Robert, who was to become the favourite of Queen Elizabeth and created Earl of Leicester, and Ambrose, who was advanced by a new creation to the title of Earl of Warwick. Queen Elizabeth paid a visit to the castle as a guest of Ambrose in 1572. She is reported to have watched country dancing in the courtyard and was treated to a firework display in the evening. After the death of Ambrose, who died childless, the inheritance reverted to the Crown. The castle began to fall into decay until James I revived the title in 1603 and bestowed it upon Robert, Lord Rich. It stayed in his family until 1759 when Francis Greville, Baron Brooke, Earl Brook, inherited the title of Earl of Warwick.

What now survives is one of the largest continuously-inhabited castles in England and one of Britain's top visitor attractions. Home of the Earl of Warwick, whose ancestors made a great impact on the course of medieval history, the castle embodies all the features of an English fortress and the spacious elegance of a 17th century mansion. Over recent years various three-dimensional displays have been added to help relate the history of the turbulent Wars of the Roses, as well as the feel of a Royal Weekend Party in 1898. One of the most scenic views of the castle is from the bridge over the River Avon.

The Collegiate Church of St Mary, Warwick CV34 4RA (D12)
Tel: 01926 403940

From the early 12th century, St Mary's became the most important church in Warwickshire, due to the patronage of local earls. The first Norman earl of Warwick, Henry de Newburgh, began a collegiate foundation, modelled on secular cathedrals, with a dean and seven canons. This was completed by his son, Roger, in 1123. During the reign of Edward III, the earldom passed into the hands of the Beauchamp family. Thomas Beauchamp planned to replace the 12th century church with a much larger edifice but died in 1369, living only long enough to see the original crypt extended. His tomb can be seen in the chancel which, along with the body of the church, was rebuilt by his son, who succeeded him as Earl Thomas II.

The final phase of medieval building was the Lady Chapel, built in accordance with the will of Richard Beauchamp, the fifth Earl and successor to Earl Thomas II, who held the title from 1401–39. (He is the 'Warwick' in *Henry IV, Part I*). Beauchamp's idea was to house, in the chapel, a magnificent gilded bronze effigy of himself, reclining on a marble tomb bearing reliefs of mourners. Some of these characters are familiar from Shakespeare's history plays, such as Stafford and Richard Neville, Earl of Warwick. For this was the Earl of Warwick who was tutor to Henry VI and appears in Shakespeare's *Henry VI, Parts II & III*. Unfortunately, the chapel was not consecrated until 1475. Also to be seen is the ornate tomb of Robert Dudley, Earl of Leicester, his wife, and their sons, Robert and Ambrose. The chapel is perhaps better-known as the Beauchamp Chapel and is arguably the finest chantry chapel in England, with wonderful Perpendicular architecture and stained-glass windows.

In 1694, a great fire destroyed the centre of Warwick, including the nave, transepts and tower of St Mary's. A major reconstruction project was put in hand and work took twelve years to complete. Rebuilding was mainly in late Gothic style. The tower of 174 feet high, rebuilt from advice by Wren's master-mason at St Paul's Cathedral – Edward Strong – was saved from crashing into the nave, which prompted its re-orientation towards Old Square. It can be seen for miles around and provides Warwick with its best landmark and one of England's finest parish churches.

Lord Leycester Hospital, 60 High Street, Warwick CV34 4BH (D12)
Tel: 01926 491422

Lovers of Tudor buildings should try and see Lord Leycester's Hospital adjacent to Warwick's Norman West Gate. It is situated in a range of picturesque half-timbered buildings, dating from the late 15th century. They originally belonged to three guilds – the Holy Trinity, the Blessed Virgin, and St George – until the Dissolution of the Monasteries. For a time, it was the premises of the local grammar school. However, in 1571 it became the property of Robert Dudley, Earl of Leicester, who turned it into a hospital for twelve men – veteran soldiers from Warwickshire and Gloucestershire – and also for one or two of his estate workers. Residents wore a uniform hat with blue gown, encapsulating a badge of the Dudley 'bear and ragged staff' crest, presented to him by Queen Elizabeth I. Today's counterparts still wear these outfits at official engagements. The complex is open to the public, who can view the Chantry Chapel, Great Hall, galleries, courtyard, Guildhall and the restored Master's Garden. The Hospital has featured in several television series including *Pride and Prejudice, Moll Flanders* and *Tom Jones*.

Wiltshire

Salisbury SP1 1EJ (B2)
Tel: 01722 334956 – Salisbury TIC

Richard III, Act 5, Scene 1

The setting for this scene is specified in the play as 'An open space, Salisbury', where Buckingham is being led to execution. In reality, Buckingham was beheaded in Salisbury's market place (B2) in 1483. He had been a supporter of Richard, Duke of York's claim to the throne but, shortly after his coronation, the King turned against Buckingham, accusing him of treason. It is said he was betrayed by a farm labourer who noticed an unusual amount of food being delivered to his hiding place. Markets have been held on the site since 1227.

Yorkshire

Middleham Castle, Castle Hill, Middleham, Leyburn, North Yorkshire DL8 (E1)

Tel: 01969 623899

Henry VI, Part III, Act 4, Scene 5

'A Park near Middleham Castle'(E1) is the setting for this particular scene. The present castle was begun in 1190 and built in the motte and bailey style. One of its most prominent inhabitants was Richard Neville, Earl of Warwick, who held both Edward IV and Henry VI prisoner at Middleham. It was here that Richard, Duke of York (later Richard III), met his future wife, Anne Neville – Warwick's daughter – whom he married in 1472. During his time at Middleham, Richard increased its importance by making it his political power base, from where he administered the North on behalf of his brother, Edward IV. When Edward died, he left two sons, Edward and Richard, who became known as the 'Princes in the Tower'. Edward, the elder, succeeded as Edward V, under the guardianship of his uncle Richard, who was appointed Protector of the Realm. Within weeks, the young king was deposed and, with his brother, was sent to the Tower of London, from which they never came out alive. A popular theory is that they were murdered on the orders of their uncle, Richard, who wished to usurp the throne. He became king in 1483 but his only son, Edward, died the following year and is buried in the parish church at Sheriff Hutton near York. King Richard was slaughtered at Bosworth Field in 1485. A contemporary statue of Richard III has been sited in the Inner Bailey of Middleham Castle.

Pontefract Castle, Castle Chain, Pontefract, West Yorkshire WF8 1BA (E12)

Tel: 01977 723440

Richard II, Act 5, Scene 5 & Richard III, Act 3, Scene 3

Shakespeare refers to this site as 'Pomfret Castle' in both plays. In *Richard II*, the overthrown Richard waits in his cell to discover his final destiny, reflecting on his wasted life. He attacks a small group of henchmen who enter the cell, killing two of them, before his own life is taken. In reality, Richard was put (or starved) to death by order of Bolingbroke at Pontefract Castle (E12). Prior to this, Richard had created

his son, Edward, as Prince of Wales on 24 August 1483, the boy having come from Middleham Castle to join his parents before their royal
entry into York. ('Pomfret Castle' is also featured in *Richard III* as the
place of execution of the lords Rivers, Grey and Vaughan.)

Edward IV stayed at the castle before the Battle of Towton. After
Richard II's death the fortress was retained as Crown property but suffered three sieges during the Civil Wars and was almost demolished.
Fragments of the elevated castle still remain and are just a five minute
walk from the town's market place. There is a visitor centre, with
daily trips to the castle cellars, once used as a dungeon. Pontefract is
well signposted from the junction of the A1 with the M62 motorway
and is reached along the A64.

Sandal Castle, Manygates Lane, Sandal Magna, Wakefield WF2 (E13)
Tel: 01924 305000 – Wakefield TIC

Henry VI, Part III, Scenes 2–4

Fresh from winning the Battle of St Albans, Richard, Duke of York, is
on the brink of seizing the throne, when Henry VI arrives and commands him to retract. York refuses. After Henry suggests that York
and his heirs succeed him, York agrees, outraging Queen Margaret,
who accuses Henry of disinheriting his own son, the Prince of Wales.
Scene 2 is actually set at Sandal Castle (E13) whereas Scenes 3 & 4 are
on a nearby battlefield. It is at the castle that York's sons persuade
their father to 'be king or die.' On 30 December 1460 York was cut
off whilst assisting a group of his men with collecting supplies from
elsewhere. They were attacked by Lancastrian forces based at nearby
Pontefract Castle under Henry Percy, Duke of Northumberland. The
Yorkists were heavily outnumbered and completely taken by surprise.
Richard decided to leave the relative safety of the castle and attack this
considerably larger and much better prepared army. He led the charge
down the castle hill but his army was heavily defeated. He died in the
battle along with over 6,000 troops.

The rhyme 'The Grand Old Duke of York', which mocks Richard
for his foolishness, is based on these events at Sandal Castle, known
as the Battle of Wakefield. In the play, the Duke of York is captured,
beheaded and, on order of the Queen, his head is sent to York for display on Micklegate Bar. The massive earthworks and ruins of Sandal
Castle have been thoroughly excavated and stand in an elevated position
high above the River Calder, giving panoramic views in all directions.

Stairways have been installed at the site to provide improved views of the castle's layout and environs. The grounds are open daily and can be visited on the western side of the village of Sandal Magna, signposted off the A61 trunk road between Barnsley and Wakefield. A visitor centre has recently been added to the site, which provides interesting background information and displays. To reach by road, exit at junction 39 of the M1 motorway and take the A636 to Wakefield. Follow A61 signs to Barnsley. Sandal Castle is signposted to the right after about half a mile and situated up Manygates Lane. An iron railing enclosure along this lane marks the spot where Richard reputedly fell.

Site of the Battle of Towton, nr Sherburn-in-Elmet, West Yorkshire LS25 (E11)
Tel: 01757 212181 – Selby TIC

Henry VI, Part III, Act 2, Scene 3

The Lancastrians routed the Yorkists at Wakefield in 1460 when the Duke of York was slain. In the following year, York's son, Edward, and Richard Neville, Earl of Warwick, turned the tables and defeated the Lancastrians at Towton (E11). Henry VI, his wife, Margaret of Anjou, and their little son, Edward, fled to Scotland. It has been estimated that up to 30,000 were slain in the battle, a decisive Yorkist victory. The battle is depicted in Scene 3 and the event commemorated by a monument situated by a signposted side road to the west of the A162, five miles (8km) south of Tadcaster.

York, North Yorkshire YO1 (E10)
Tel: 01904 621756 – York TIC

Henry VI, Part III, Act 4, Scenes 6 & 7

When Sir Henry Percy (Hotspur) was defeated and killed at the Battle of Shrewsbury in 1403, his body was quartered and pieces despatched to different parts of England as evidence of his defeat. His head was sent to York (E10), where it was displayed on a spike at Micklegate Bar as a warning to other Yorkshire men. Much of the oak for the building of York Minster came from the estates of the Percy family. A statue of Henry Percy, 3rd Baron of Alnwick (1322–68), can be seen in the south side of the Lady Chapel; a retrospective memorial denoting his contribution to the construction of the chapel and his outstanding generosity. (York Minster – Tel: 01904 557216)

In Scene 6, King Henry VI names the young Earl of Richmond as the future Henry VII outside the Tower of London. In Scene 7, Edward, Prince of Wales, enters York as King Edward IV, along with Richard, Duke of Gloucester, and Lord Hastings. They are met by the Mayor of York and his brethren on the city walls, built in Roman times, which still encircle this beautiful and historic city. There is an excellent small museum in the Monkbar, dedicated to the life of Richard III (Tel: 01904 634191).

Scotland

Macbeth

Much of Shakespeare's play *Macbeth* is based on pure fiction and bears little resemblance to facts known about the real Macbeth. His character has been much maligned by the play, originally written for James I after he united Scotland with England under the one crown in 1603. Will wrote the play to flatter the new monarch and its first performance was given in his presence at Hampton Court in August 1605. As with other of Shakespeare's plays, it is sometimes hard to separate fact from fiction, so a short appraisal is given to illustrate how such a drama was evolved from somewhat doubtful origins.

Earlier chroniclers brought about major misunderstandings of Macbeth through efforts to establish an unbroken line of Scottish kings back to the 6th century. These writers included John of Fordoun (died 1387), Walter Bower (15th century) and Hector Boece (died 1536). The English historian Holinshed copied passages from the last-named and Will used these as a basis for his play. This gave legitimacy both to the King of Scots and to the Stewarts. James's own line went back through Duncan and Malcolm Canmore rather than Macbeth. Thus, Macbeth appears as a villainous character in the play.

Though he is described by Shakespeare as Thane of Glamis and Thane of Cawdor, there is little evidence to support the Glamis link, and Cawdor Castle was not built until some centuries after Macbeth's death. Neither was Duncan murdered there. In truth, the real Macbeth is thought to have been an able monarch who ruled for 17 years. Duncan was most likely wounded in battle against Macbeth and died at or close to Spynie Palace *(HS)*, near Elgin (F8). Macbeth's wife (real name Gruoch) was not the schemer depicted in the play; neither was she insane. As in the play, Macbeth's troops were indeed attacked at Dunsinane near Balbeggie, but in reality he survived. Three years later, Malcolm Canmore took an army to Scotland and defeated and killed

Macbeth at Lymphanan, Aberdeenshire, in August 1057. The general opinion is that Scotland had become a prosperous nation under him. Macbeth strengthened the rule of law to create greater discipline and control among his subjects. He even made a Christian pilgrimage to Rome.

Scone Palace, Perth, Perthshire PH2 6BD (F3)
Tel: 01738 552300

Stone of Scone

Scone is a castellated palace, enlarged and embellished in 1803, incorporating several earlier palaces. Scone Palace (F3) is the home of the Earl of Mansfield and was an early site of coronations of kings of Scotland and of Scottish Parliaments, on Moot (or Boot) Hill. An artificial mound was created by earth brought in the boots of lords swearing loyalty to their king. (In Act 2, Scene 4 of the play, Macduff remarks to Ross that Macbeth has gone to Scone to be crowned.) There is a replica of the stone upon which kings of Scotland were crowned on Moot Hill until 1296, after which Edward I removed the 'Stone of Scone' to Westminster Abbey. It is now back in Scotland and kept at Edinburgh Castle along with the 'honours of Scotland'. To reach Scone Palace, take the A93 road from Perth to Blairgowrie and proceed for 2 miles (3km), following signs for the palace. Moot Hill is clearly indicated in the grounds.

Birnam Wood, Dunkeld, Perthshire PH8 (F4)
Tel: 01350 727688 – Dunkeld TIC

From the A9 trunk road, take the Birnam (F4) exit into the town to follow a woodland walk to see the reputed remaining oak tree from the original wood in Shakespeare's play. Historians claim the wood was used to camouflage Malcolm Canmore's army before their battle with Macbeth at Dunsinane. (This is referred to in Act 5, Scene 4 of the drama).

Dunsinane Hill, nr Balbeggie, Perthshire PH2 (F5)
Tel: 01350 727688 – Dunkeld TIC

This is one of the Sidlaw Hills and situated 15 miles (24km) south east of Birnam Wood. Follow the A94 from Perth through New Scone and turn right at Balbeggie on to the B953. Dunsinane Hill (F5) is about 3 miles (5km) from the turning. A footpath leads to the summit at 1,000 feet, which involves a steep climb to the site of an Iron Age fort and a panoramic view of the surrounding area. The fort is known as Macbeth's Castle and is where, by tradition, he awaited Canmore's troops from Birnam. According to Act 5, Scene 7, Macbeth was killed there.

Glamis Castle, Glamis, by Forfar, Angus DD8 1RJ (F6)
Tel: 01307 840393

Glamis Castle (F6) was the childhood home of the late Queen Mother, birthplace of the late Princess Margaret, and where Malcolm II is said to have died in 1034. In the old keep is Duncan's Hall, but any connection to the king is through Shakespeare's play. It can be reached off the A928, just over 5 miles (8km) south west of Forfar.

Inverness (F9)
Tel: 01463 234353 – Inverness TIC

In Act 1, Scenes 5–7 and Act 2, Scenes 1–3, the setting is Macbeth's Castle at Inverness, which is also the place where Duncan is murdered in the play. The original castle was blown up at the Jacobite rebellion in 1746 and was replaced in 1835 by a mock castle on the same site (the present Inverness Castle). This is not thought to be the site of the one referred to by Shakespeare, which is supposed to have been half a mile east of the town. Malcolm Canmore is said to have destroyed a castle of Macbeth's at Inverness in 1057, thought to be at this location. There is no trace of this fortification and the site is now occupied by houses.

Macbeth's Hillock, Moray IV36 (F9)
Tel: 01309 672938 – Forres TIC

This traditional site is situated about a quarter of a mile north of the A96 at Easter Hardmuir, between Forres and Nairn, just west of Brodie Castle. Macbeth's Hillock (F9) is the reputed site of the track being travelled by Macbeth and Banquo when they were confronted by the three witches at the start of the play.

Cawdor Castle, Nairn IV12 5RD (F10)
Tel: 01667 404401

Cawdor Castle (F10) was built some centuries after the death of Macbeth. Its medieval tower and drawbridge are still intact. The castle is situated 5 miles (8km) south west of Nairn on B9090 off the A96.

Banquo's Walk, nr Fort William, Highland (F11)
Tel: 01397 702169 – West Highland Museum

This is a beautiful secluded woodland avenue by the banks of the River Lochy near Fort William, known for years as Banquo's Walk (F11). Turn off the A830 Fort William to Mallaig road and right on the B8004, passing Neptune's Staircase (a series of locks on the Caledonian Canal). Continue to Muirshearlich and turn right at the restaurant. Continue on foot along track and through tunnel, leading to the walk.

Macbeth's Death Site – Lumphanan, Kincardine & Deeside (F7)
Tel: 01224 288828 – Aberdeen TIC

In Shakespeare's play Macbeth dies at Dunsinane Castle but, according to tradition, he was actually slain in battle by Malcolm's troops at Lumphanan (F7) in 1057, and his body was taken to Iona. Lumphanan is situated by the River Dee, just off the A93, five miles (8km) north east of Aboyne. At this site are a large boulder named Macbeth's Stone – thought to be where he died – and Macbeth's Well, where he drank prior to the battle. Nearby is Macbeth's Cairn – the traditional site of the King's burial prior to his body being transferred to Iona.

Macbeth's Last Resting Place, Iona Abbey (HS), Isle of Iona,
via Mull PA76 6SQ (F12)
Tel: 08707 200 630 – Oban TIC

The traditional burial place of early kings of Scotland, including Macbeth and Duncan, is the graveyard of Iona Abbey (F12). To reach Iona, travel to the Isle of Mull by ferry on either the Oban to Craignure or the Lochaline to Fishnish line, then go by coach or car to Fionnphort and take a short ferry crossing to Iona. (No cars on Iona.) From here, it is a short walk to the abbey and royal burial ground.

Here's the smell of the blood still
All the perfumes of Arabia will not sweeten this little hand.
Oh, oh, oh!

Macbeth, Act 5, Scene 1

Edward III

In Act 1, scenes are set in both London and the Scottish Borders. Word reaches the English capital that King David of Scotland has set his sights on England and is besieging the Countess of Salisbury in Roxburgh Castle (F2), where he tries to woo the fair lady. Act 2 is set in Roxburgh. The play was long thought to have been written in the early 1590s by a person or persons other than Shakespeare, until recent research was undertaken. However, it is still held that Shakespeare only wrote part of it – it is recognised as a collaboration between Will Shakespeare and one (or more) other(s). Will is believed to have written the scenes with the Countess in Act 1 and the work has now been added to Shakespeare's other plays. It did not prove popular at Elizabeth's court due to its treatment of the Scots, especially as James VI was likely to become the Queen's successor.

For a hundred years, from the mid-14th century, Roxburgh Castle was held by the English. James II of Scotland resolved to win it back for the Scots. On Sunday 3 August 1460 he was supervising the discharge of a great gun towards the castle when it exploded and killed him. His widow, Mary of Guelders, made her way to the Scots camp with her eight-year-old son and inspired the soldiers to continue their assault to a successful conclusion. However, on second thoughts, she realised its continued existence was a threat – despite its original purpose as a guard of Scottish safety. She duly had the castle demolished.

Roxburgh Castle, Roxburgh, Scottish Borders (F2)
Tel: 01835 863688 – Jedburgh TIC

Earthworks are all that remain of the once mighty fortress and walled Royal Burgh which gave its name to the former county. The present village of Roxburgh dates from a later period. The castle site is off the A699, 1 mile (1.5km) south west of Kelso. Access at all times.

Wales

Richard II and Henry IV, Part I

In Act 3 of *Richard II,* Henry Bolingbroke incurs the mistrust of the King on suspicion of his involvement in a plot to overthrow him. By Scene 2, the King knows the situation is grave. Richard confiscates his lands and property and takes his sons as hostages. In 1398, he sentenced Bolingbroke to ten years exile, which was later extended to banishment. (In the play, he sentences him to ten years, then reduces it to six. However, he tries to seize Bolingbroke's estate to raise money for the Irish wars, leading, in part, to Bolingbroke's return and subsequent rebellion.) Whilst the King was on a mission to Ireland, Bolingbroke took advantage of his absence and sailed to Boulogne to reclaim his inheritance. He arrived back in England in July 1399, prompting Richard to return hurriedly to North Wales, where he received much personal support. He arrived at Conwy (E9) and was met by the Earl of Northumberland, to whom he had earlier granted the custody of Flint Castle. He was informed that Bolingbroke, encamped at Chester, was seeking a meeting. Shortly afterwards, King Richard was ambushed and escorted to Rhuddlan Castle, then back to Flint Castle and into the hands of Bolingbroke. The King was imprisoned in the Tower of London and compelled to sign a deed of abdication in favour of Bolingbroke, who was then crowned Henry IV.

Flint Castle (E8) was built by Edward I in 1277 and completed in 1286. Whilst in France, he founded 49 planned towns in the duchy of Gascony. He later followed suit at Flint and set a trend for his other Welsh castles, combining the castle with the new fortified town in one defensive unit.

Flint Castle, Flint, Clwyd CH6 (E8)
Tel: 01352 7599331 – Mold TIC

The ruined sandstone castle in the small town of Flint sits on a low promontory bordering the shores of the River Dee. It consisted of an inner bailey with three circular towers and an offset tower, the Donjon, built beyond the curved wall of the south eastern corner. The outer bailey has now almost disappeared. The castle is on the A548, ten miles (16km) from Chester and open at all reasonable hours.

Denmark

Elsinore

Tel: 0045 4921 3078 – Kronberg Castle

Hamlet

Shakespeare's story of *Hamlet, Prince of Denmark* takes place behind the walls of Elsinore's castle. Kronberg, completed 1585, is therefore known throughout the world as Hamlet's castle and Elsinore – Helsinger, in North Zealand – as Hamlet's town. When Will wrote the play in 1601 he used Kronberg Castle as the setting but there is no evidence he ever visited the place. It is known, however, that several actors from Britain performed at both Kronberg and Elsinore and it is possible they described the majestic castle to Shakespeare back in England.

Elsinore is 22 miles (35km) north of Copenhagen, and has long been a busy port, with regular ferries to and from Sweden. Visitors are taken on a tour of the castle, which has a portrait of Shakespeare on a stone tablet at the main entrance. Of special interest is a *Hamlet* exhibition which describes the tradition for performances at Kronberg, and the range of interpretations of the play since 1816. The Danish Maritime Museum is housed at the same site, at what is acknowledged to be one of the most important Renaissance castles in Northern Europe. Kronberg is situated 1km from Helsinger railway station.

France

Site of Battle of Agincourt, Picardy

Tel: +33 (0)3 21 04 41 12 – Visitor Centre

Henry V

Henry, Prince of Wales (later King Henry v), at the age of 16, led his father's forces to a decisive victory at the battle of Shrewsbury. When he succeeded the throne in 1413, the young Henry set his sights on France. He attacked the port of Harfleur in 1415. Marching an army through France, he was arrested by a 50,000-strong French force at Agincourt. Against all odds, the French army was forcibly defeated and Henry went on to claim Normandy, Touraine and Maine, among other French regions. He was a talented soldier with a brilliant tactical mind. In 1420 he was recognised as heir to the French crown. However, two years later he was struck down with dysentery and died.

The village of Azincourt lies 11 miles (18km) from the town of Hesdin, north of Abbeville, south of St Omer, and is best approached via the D104 from Blagny. It is only accessible by road. The Agincourt Battlefield lies within a triangle of land between the three villages of Azincourt, Trâmecourt and Maisoncelles, where a cruciform, erected 1963, recalls the historic episode. Near to the village of Azincourt is the Centre Historique Médiéval d'Azincourt, which shows documents relating to the battle, along with photographs, copies of arms and armour, and models of weaponry used. An orientation map is available, and there is a clearly-marked two mile (3km) trail around the battlefield, leading from the visitor centre.

Italy

The House of Desdemona, Venice

Tel: +39 0415 298711 – Venice Tourist Information

Othello

According to legend, the Palazzo Contarini-Fasan on Venice's Grand Canal was the house of Desdemona, a noble Venetian lady who fell victim to the mad jealousy of her husband, a member of the Moro family. Shakespeare made her his tragic heroine in *Othello*. The house is located on Canalazzo – Venice's main thoroughfare – with its facade overlooking the Grand Canal. It can be reached by waterbus (Vaporettostop) from Santa Maria del Giglio. Other important buildings include the Duomo of San Marco, built on the site of a chapel to which the body of St Mark was brought from Alexandria in 828 AD. The Doges Palace adjoins San Marco and was begun in 1300.

The Rialto Bridge, Venice

Tel: +39 0415 298711 – Venice Tourist Information

The Merchant of Venice

The graceful bridge, halfway along the canal, was built between 1588 and 1591 by Antonio da Ponte, and was designed to allow an armed galley to pass under it. Traditionally, it divides the city into halves. It is a strong, elegantly curved arch of marble, with a central street lined with shops and gangways affording majestic views of the Grand Canal. In Act 1, Scene 3 Shylock speaks his famous line to Bassanio: 'What news on the Rialto? Who is he comes here?' This line may refer to the bridge, or to the exchange of the same name where Venetian gentlemen and merchants met to discuss business.

Romeo and Juliet, Two Gentlemen of Verona & The Taming of the Shrew

The House of Capulet & Juliet's Balcony, Verona
Tel: +39 045 806 8680 – Verona Tourism

Juliet's Balcony

Verona was the setting for *Romeo and Juliet*, which took place in 1302. The star-cross'd lovers belonged to rival families – Romeo to the Montagues, who supported the Pope, and Juliet to the Capulets, who supported the Emperor. In the Via Cappello (No. 23) is Juliet's House (Casa di Giulietta), a Gothic palace (with the famous 'Juliet's Balcony' in its inner courtyard) which belonged to the Capulet family. Today, visitors stand in the courtyard and gaze up towards the celebrated balcony – a symbol of love throughout the world. The original tomb of Juliet has long since been destroyed but a modern substitute has been provided in the cloisters of the Church of San Francesco al Corsontiere, situated at Via del Pontiere 35, in which Romeo and Juliet were married. The memorial is a marble sarcophagus made in the 14th century.

The scene of the *Two Gentlemen of Verona* is set at first in this city but, afterwards, moves to Milan. In *The Taming of the Shrew*, Petruchio says 'I am a gentleman of Verona' and his country house, in which some of the later scenes are set, is probably situated near the city.

The Roman Forum and Capitol, Rome
Tel: +39 06 3996 7700 – Tourist Information

Coriolanus, Julius Caesar & Titus Andronicus

According to legend Romulus and Remus founded Rome around the year 750 BC, but this cannot be proven. Scholars now think that the Etruscans, a race of superb soldier-craftsmen, had a profound influence on Rome's formative years. The city's last king, Tarquin the Proud, was expelled in 510 BC and the city became a republic ruled by the Senate and the people. There followed rapid expansion and Rome swiftly extended its borders, absorbing the rest of Italy and then Sicily, Carthage, Spain and Greece. The hub of Roman life was the Forum; the political, administrative and religious centre of Rome.

The Forum underwent several refurbishments, notably when it was lined with columns in the second century BC. Around it stood the High Priest's House, the dwelling of the Vestal Virgins, and the Senate. Rome was the setting for three of Shakespeare's plays, *Coriolanus* (493 BC), *Julius Caesar* (44 BC) and *Titus Andronicus* (no set date). Winding across the site was the Via Sacra, a triumphal route which led from the Forum to the Temple of Jupiter on the Capitol. Julius Caesar built a new Forum to the north of the old one. Later emperors followed his trend, striving to outdo their predecessors in magnificence by building splendid palaces on the Palatine Hill. There were other projects, such as the Circus Maximus, once used for chariot-racing, the Theatre of Marcellus, and the awesome Colosseum, where early Christians were fed to wild animals.

For today's visitor, there is something desolate about the whole scene, with its ruins of grandeur. But with a bit of imagination, one can easily create an impression of what the mighty Roman Empire must have been like in its glory days.

The Capitoline Hill, the smallest of Rome's seven hills, has been the focus of political power over the centuries. It offers excellent views across the Forum. The city council still occupies the Palazzo Senatorio, the seat of government, atop the Capitoline. Close by are the Palazzo Nuovo and Palazzo dei Conservatori, which are together known as the Musei Capitolini. The complex of buildings is approached along a graceful ramp, known as the Cardonata, just off Piazza Venezia. There is much to see, from classical sculpture to priceless paintings by famous artists depicting scenes from Rome's glorious past.

Our revels now are ended. These our actors,
As I foretold you, were all spirits, and
Are melted into air, into thin air;
And like the baseless fabric of this vision,
The cloud-capped towers, the gorgeous palaces,
The solemn temples, the great globe itself,
Yea, all which it inherit, shall dissolve;
And like this insubstantial pageant faded,
Leave not a rack behind. We are such stuff
As dreams are made on, and our little life
Is rounded with a sleep.

The Tempest, Act 4, Scene 1

Chronology of Shakespeare's Times

1550 (circa)	John Shakespeare (father) moves from Snitterfield to Stratford-upon-Avon.
1557	John Shakespeare marries Mary Arden, possibly at Aston Cantlow.
1558	Accession of Elizabeth I to the throne of England on the death of Mary Tudor.
1560	Death of Richard Shakespeare (grandfather). Buried at Snitterfield.
1564 – circa 23 April	Birth of William Shakespeare at Henley Street, Stratford-upon-Avon.
– 26 April	Shakespeare baptized at Holy Trinity Church, Stratford-upon-Avon.
	War ends between France and England; Christopher Marlowe, dramatist, born.
1565 – 4 Sept	John Shakespeare elected alderman of Stratford-upon-Avon.
1566 – 19 June	Mary Queen of Scots gives birth to James – future James VI of Scotland and James I of England – at Edinburgh Castle.
1567	Richard Burbage, actor, born.
	Abdication of Mary Queen of Scots from the throne of Scotland in favour of her son, James, who becomes King James VI of Scotland.
1568 – 4 Sept	John Shakespeare elected bailiff of Stratford-upon-Avon.
	Mary Queen of Scots flees to England.
1569	Uprising by Northern Earls in favour of Roman Catholicism.
1570	Pope Pius excommunicates Elizabeth I.
1572	Ben Jonson, dramatist, born. Burghley becomes Lord Treasurer.

1573	Francis Walsingham becomes Principal Secretary.
1574	First seminary priests arrive in England.
1575	Elizabeth I attends theatrical performances at Kenilworth Castle.
1576	James Burbage opens The Theatre, Shoreditch, London.
1577	John Shakespeare ceases to attend council meetings due to bankruptcy; the Curtain theatre opened in London; Francis Drake starts his circumnavigation of the world.
1579 – 4 April	Shakespeare's sister, Anne, dies and is buried at Holy Trinity Church.
1580	First Jesuit mission arrives in England; Drake completes circumnavigation of the world.
1582 – 28 Nov	License issued in Worcester for the marriage of William Shakespeare and Anne Hathaway. The location of the wedding ceremony is unknown, but may have been at Temple Grafton.
1583 – 26 May	Shakespeare's first child, Susanna, is baptised at Holy Trinity Church.
1584	Throckmorton Plot uncovered (a Catholic plot to assassinate Queen Elizabeth and replace her with Mary Queen of Scots).
1585 – 2 Feb	Baptism of Hamnet and Judith, William and Anne's twins.
1587 – 8 Feb	Execution of Mary Queen of Scots at Fotheringhay Castle. Rose theatre opens in Bankside, London; The Queen's Men and Leicester's Men theatre companies perform in Stratford-upon-Avon. Shakespeare reputedly moved to London with one of the companies around this time.
1588	Defeat of Spanish Armada; death of Robert

	Dudley, Earl of Leicester – buried in St Mary's Church, Warwick.
	Earl of Leicester's Men merge with Lord Strange's Men. They play mainly at The Theatre and the Rose.
1590	*Henry VI, Part 1*
	Death of Walsingham – Elizabeth's master 'Spy Catcher.'
1591	*Henry VI, Parts 2 & 3*
1592–94	Outbreak of plague closes London theatres.
1593	*Richard III*, **'Venus and Adonis' – narrative poem**
	Christopher Marlowe dies.
1594	*Edward III, Titus Andronicus, The Comedy of Errors, The Taming of the Shrew, The Two Gentlemen of Verona,* **'The Rape of Lucrece' – narrative poem**
	Admiral's Men at Rose Playhouse.
1595	*Love's Labour's Lost, Richard II*
	Swan Playhouse built at Bankside, London.
1596	*Romeo and Juliet, A Midsummer Night's Dream, King John*
– 11 Aug	Hamnet Shakespeare, son, dies aged 11.
	Shakespeare living in parish of St Helen's, Bishopgate, London; James Burbage buys Blackfriars property; death of Sir Francis Drake.
– 20 Oct	Grant of Arms to John Shakespeare.
1597	*The Merchant of Venice, Henry IV, Part 1*
– May	Shakespeare buys New Place, Stratford-upon-Avon; James Burbage dies and his property is inherited by his son, Richard.
	Newly-formed Lord Chamberlain's Men play mainly at The Theatre and Shakespeare becomes a leading shareholder in the Company.

1598	*Henry IV, Part 2*
	Death of Lord Burghley; The Theatre at Blackfriars dismantled, and rebuilt at Bankside. It is renamed the Globe and Shakespeare and colleagues named as shareholders.
1599	*Henry V, Much Ado About Nothing, Julius Caesar, As You Like It*
	Opening of the Globe; Edmund Spencer dies; birth of Oliver Cromwell.
1601	*Hamlet*
	John Shakespeare dies. Buried at Holy Trinity Church.
1602	*Twelfth Night, The Merry Wives of Windsor*
1603	*All's Well That Ends Well*
	Elizabeth I dies. She is succeeded by James VI of Scotland as James I of England; the Chamberlain's Men re-named the King's Men.
1603-04	London theatres closed as 30,000 die of plague; Shakespeare living in parish of St Olave, Cripplegate, London.
1604	*Othello, Measure for Measure*
1605	*King Lear*
	Discovery of 'Gunpowder Plot' to assassinate King James at Westminster.
1606	*Macbeth*
	The King's Men act Ben Jonson's *Volpone* at the Globe.
1607 – 5 June	Marriage of Shakespeare's elder daughter, Susanna, to Dr John Hall, at Holy Trinity Church.
– 31 Dec	Shakespeare's youngest brother, Edmund, buried in St Saviour's Church, Southwark (now Southwark Cathedral).
1608	*Pericles, Coriolanus, Timon of Athens,*

	Troilus and Cressida, Anthony and Cleopatra
– 21 Feb	Elizabeth Hall (Susanna's baby daughter) baptized at Holy Trinity Church.
– 9 Sept	Mary Shakespeare (mother) buried at Holy Trinity Church.
	The King's Men take over Blackfriars Theatre.
1609	*Sonnets* published
1610	*Cymbeline*
	Shakespeare thought to have returned to live at New Place, Stratford-upon-Avon.
1611	*The Winter's Tale, The Tempest*
	Authorised Version of the Bible published.
1613	*Henry VIII*
– 29 June	The Globe is burnt down.
	Shakespeare buys property in Blackfriars.
1614	*Cardenio* (since lost)*, The Two Noble Kinsmen*
– 30 June	Re-built Globe re-opens.
1616 – 10 Feb	Judith Shakespeare (younger daughter) marries Thomas Quiney.
– 25 Mar	Shakespeare makes his will.
– 23 Apr	Death of William Shakespeare. Buried at Holy Trinity Church two days later.
1623	*First Folio* published
	Death of Anne Shakespeare (wife). Buried at Holy Trinity Church.

Useful Addresses

BRITAIN

Tourist Information

(It is advisable before visiting any sites or venues to check days and times of opening with the actual site or with the local tourist information centre.)

VisitBritain
Thames Tower
Black's Road
London W6 9EL
Tel: 020 8846 9000
www.visitbritain.com

Churches Conservation Trust
1 West Smithfield
London EC1A 9EE
Tel: 020 7213 0660
www.visitchurches.org.uk

English Heritage
PO Box 569
Swindon SN2 2YP
Tel: 0870 333 1182
www.english-heritage.org.uk

The National Trust
36 Queen Anne's Gate
London SW1H 9AS
Tel: 0870 609 5380
www.nationaltrust.org.uk

Heart of England Tourism
Larkhill Road
Worcester WR5 2EZ
Tel: 01905 761100
www.visitheartofengland.com

Heart of England Tourist Guides Association
Tel: 0121 711 3225

South Warwickshire Tourism
3 Trinity Mews, Priory Road,
Warwick CV34 4NA
www.shakespeare-country.co.uk

Tourist Information Centre
The Library
Smalley Place
Kenilworth CV8 1QG
Tel: 01926 748900

Tourist Information Centre
The Royal Pump Rooms
The Parade
Royal Leamington Spa CV32 4AB
Tel: 01926 742762
Email:
leamington@shakespeare-country.co.uk

Tourist Information Centre
Bridgefoot
Stratford-upon-Avon CV37 6GW
Tel: 0870 160 7930
Email:
stratfordtic@shakespeare-country.co.uk

Tourist Information Centre
Jury Street
Warwick CV34 4EW
Tel: 01926 492212
www.warwick-uk.co.uk

Tourist Information Centre
The Guildhall
High Street
Worcester WR1 2EY
Tel: 01905 726311
Email:
touristinfo@cityofworcester.gov.uk

STRATFORD–UPON–AVON

City Sightseeing (Open top bus tours)
Juliette Way
Purfleet Industrial Park
Purfleet, Essex RM15 4YA
Tel: 01708 865656
Email: info@city-sightseeing.com

Guide Friday Ltd (Open top bus tours)
Civic Hall
14 Rother Street
Stratford-upon-Avon CV37 6LU
Tel: 01789 294466
Email: info@guidefriday.com

Holy Trinity Church
Old Town
Stratford-upon-Avon CV37 6BG
Tel: 01789 266316
Email:
office@stratford-upon-avon.org

Shakespeare Birthplace Trust Records Office
Henley Street
Stratford-upon-Avon CV37 6QW
Tel: 01789 201816/204016
E-mail: records@shakespeare.org.uk

The Shakespeare Houses (marked *SH*) –
c/o The Shakespeare Centre
Henley Street
Stratford-upon-Avon CV37 6QW
Tel: 01789 201806/201836
www.shakespeare.org.uk

Shakespeare's Birthplace & Exhibition *SH*
Henley Street
Stratford-upon-Avon
Tel: 01789 201823

Anne Hathaway's Cottage *SH*
Shottery
Stratford-upon-Avon
Tel: 01789 292100

Mary Arden's House *SH*
Wilmcote
nr Stratford-upon-Avon
Tel: 01789 293455

Hall's Croft *SH*
Old Town
Stratford-upon-Avon
Tel: 01789 292107

Harvard House *SH*
High Street
Stratford-upon-Avon
Tel: 01789 204016

Nash's House & New Place *SH*
Chapel Street
Stratford-upon-Avon
Tel: 01789 292325

The Shakespeare Institute
Church Street
Stratford-upon-Avon
Tel: 01789 293138

Royal Shakespeare Company:

Royal Shakespeare Theatre
Waterside
Stratford-upon-Avon CV37 6BB
Tel: 01789 403403
(24-hour answer phone service)
Box Office Tel: 0870 609 1110
www.rsc.org.uk

The Swan Theatre
Waterside
Stratford-upon-Avon
(See Box Office Tel. above)

The Other Place Theatre
Southern Lane
Stratford-upon-Avon
(See Box Office Tel. above)

WARWICKSHIRE

Baddesley Clinton *NT*
Rising Lane
Baddesley Clinton Village,
Knowle, Solihull B93 0DQ
Tel: 01564 783294
www.nationaltrust.org.uk

Charlecote Park *NT*
Warwick CV35 9ER
Tel: 01789 470277
www.nationaltrust.org.uk

Coughton Court *NT*
nr Alcester B49 5JA
Tel: 01789 400777
www.coughtoncourt.co.uk

Kenilworth Castle *EH*
Kenilworth CV8 1NE
Tel: 01926 852078
www.english-heritage.org.uk

Packwood House *NT*
Lapworth
Solihull B94 6AT
Email: baddesleyclinton@ntrust.org.uk

Warwick Castle
Warwick CV34 4QU
Tel: 0870 442 2000
www.warwick-castle.com

WORCESTER

Worcestershire County Record Office
Spetchley Road
Worcester WR5 2NP
Tel: 01905 766351

LONDON

Shakespeare's Globe
21 New Globe Walk
London SE1 9DT
Tel: 020 7902 1400
Box Office Tel: 020 7401 9919
www.shakespeares-globe.org

Rose Theatre Exhibition
56 Park Street
London SE1
Tel: 020 7593 0026

Southwark Cathedral
Montague Close
London Bridge
London SE1 9DA
Tel: 020 7367 6700
Email: cathedral@dswark.org.uk

OTHER SITES

Bosworth Battlefield Visitor Centre
Sutton Cheney, nr Market Bosworth
Nuneaton CV13 0AD
Tel: 01455 290429
Email: bosworth@leics.gov.uk

Hoghton Tower
Hoghton
Preston
Lancashire
Tel: 01254 852 986

Battlefield Heritage Park, Shrewsbury
Countryside Service, Shropshire County
Council
Tel: 01691 624448

Church of St Mary Magdalene CCT
Battlefield, nr Shrewsbury
Shropshire
Tel: 0207 213 0660

Warkworth Castle & Hermitage EH
Warkworth, nr Alnwick
Northumberland
Tel: 01665 711 423

York Minster – Visitors' Department
St William's College
4-5 College Street
York YO1 7JF
Tel: 01904 557216
Email: visitors@yorkminster.org

SCOTLAND

Visit Scotland
23 Ravelston Terrace
Edinburgh EH4 3TP
Tel: 0131 332 2433
www.visitscotland.com

WALES

Wales Tourist Board
Brunel House, 2 Fitzalan Road
Cardiff CF24 0UY
Tel: 08708 300 306
www.visitwales.com

DENMARK

Danish Tourist Board
55 Sloane Street
London SW1X 9SY
Tel: 0900 1600109

Kronberg Castle
Kronberg 2c, DK-3000 Elsinore
Tel: Add country code then 0045 4921
    3078
Email: Kronborg@ses.dk

FRANCE

France Tourist Information
178 Piccadilly
London W1V 0AL
Tel: 020 7355 4747

ITALY

Italian Government Tourist Board
1 Princes Street
London W1B 28AY
Tel: 020 7408 1254

Bibliography

Bryson, Graham	*Shakespeare in Lancashire* Sunwards Publishing, Liverpool, 1997
Cheetham, J. Keith	*On the Trail of Mary Queen of Scots* Luath Press Ltd., Edinburgh, 1999
Dunton-Downer, Leslie & Riding, Alan	*Essential Shakespeare Handbook* Dorling Kindersley Ltd., 2004
Fox, Levi	*The Early History of King Edward VI School, Stratford-upon-Avon* The Dugdale Society, Oxford, 1984
Harrison, W. Jerome	*Shakespeare-Land* Warwickshire Books, Warwick, 1995
Holden, Anthony	*William Shakespeare, His Life and Work* Little, Brown and Company, London, 1999
Honigmann, E.A.J.	*Shakespeare: The Lost Years* Manchester University Press, Manchester, 1985
Keates, Jonathan	*The Companion Guide to the Shakespeare Country* Collins, London, 1979
Lambirth, Andrew	*William Shakespeare – A biography with the complete Sonnets* Brockhampton Press, London, 1999
Lloyd, David	*A History of Worcestershire* Phillimore & Co. Ltd., Chichester, 1993
Phillips, Graham & Keatman, Martin	*The Shakespeare Conspiracy* Century, London, 1988
Plowden, Alison	*Elizabeth Regina 1588-1603* Macmillian Ltd., London, 1980
Pringle, Marian J.	*The Theatres of Stratford-upon-Avon 1875–1992* Stratford-upon-Avon Society 1993
Quennell, Peter & Johnson, Hamish	*Who's Who in Shakespeare* Weidenfeld & Nicholson, London, 1973
Rosenthal, Daniel	*Shakespeare on Screen* Hamlyn, London, 2000
Russell Brown, John	*Shakespeare and his Theatre* Penguin Books Ltd., London, 1982

Singleton, Frank	*Hoghton Tower* Hoghton Tower Preservation Trust, 1999
Southworth, John	*Shakespeare the Player* Sutton Publishing, Stroud, 2000
Speaight, Robert	*Shakespeare – The Man and his Achievement* J.M. Dent & Sons Ltd., London, 1977
Thorndike, Russell	*A Wanderer with Shakespeare* Rich & Cowan, London, 1940
Manchester, University of	*A Topographical Dictionary to the Works of Shakespeare* Manchester University Press, 1925
WFWI	*The Warwickshire Village Book* Countryside Books, Newbury, 1988
Wells, Stanley	*Shakespeare – For All Time* Macmillan, London, 2002
Wood, Michael	*In Search of Shakespeare* BBC Worldwide Ltd., London, 2003

Some other books published by **LUATH** PRESS

On the Trail of the Pilgrim Fathers

J. Keith Cheetham
ISBN 0 946487 83 9 PBK £7.99

The fascinating, true story of the founding fathers of the United States, their origins in England and their harrowing journey to a New World.

After harvest time in 1621 around 60 men, women and children held a great feast in gratitude to God to celebrate their deliverance and the first anniversary of their leaving England to found a settlement in North America. These people became known as the Pilgrim Fathers. The feast was repeated annually and became known as Thanks-giving. Almost 400 years later, US citizens still celebrate Thanksgiving. But who were the Pilgrim Fathers?

The political situation in 16th and 17th century England was such that those who differed from the established church were persecuted, punished and humiliated. The Puritans determined to leave English shores rather than submit to changing their beliefs.

In this account, Keith Cheetham tells of their flight to Holland, their subsequent departure from Plymouth on the Mayflower in September 1620 and the perils that faced them in the New World. These are true stories of tragedy and danger as well as success.

Over 170 places to visit in England, Holland and the USA

One general map, 4 location maps of England, 1 of Holland and 1 of New England

Line drawings and illustrations

List of names of those who sailed in the Mayflower.

As in his earlier book, *On the Trail of Mary Queen of Scots*, Keith Cheetham once again gives a thorough guide to the origins and places connected with these early settlers. He sets their achievements in the context of earlier European explorers to the New World.

On the Trail of the Pilgrim Fathers is for everyone interested in the brave folk who left the Old World for the New.

On the Trail of Mary Queen of Scots

J. Keith Cheetham
ISBN 0 946487 50 2 PBK £7.99

Life dealt Mary Queen of Scots love, intrigue, betrayal and tragedy in generous measure.

On the Trail of Mary Queen of Scots traces the major events in the turbulent life of the beautiful, enigmatic queen whose romantic reign and tragic destiny exerts an undimmed fascination over 400 years after her execution.

Places of interest to visit – 99 in Scotland, 35 in England and 29 in France.

One general map and 6 location maps.

Line drawings and illustrations.

Simplified family tree of the royal houses of Tudor and Stuart.

Key sites include:

Linlithgow Palace – Mary's birthplace, now a magnificent ruin

Stirling Castle – where, only nine months old, Mary was crowned Queen of Scotland

Notre Dame Cathedral – where, aged fifteen, she married the future king of France

The Palace of Holyroodhouse – Rizzio, one of Mary's closest advisers, was murdered here and some say his blood still stains the spot where he was stabbed to death

Sheffield Castle – where for fourteen years she languished as prisoner of her cousin, Queen Elizabeth 1

Fotheringhay – here Mary finally met her death on the executioner's block.

On the Trail of Mary Queen of Scots is for everyone interested in the life of perhaps the most romantic figure in Scotland's history; a thorough guide to places connected with Mary, it is also a guide to the complexities of her personal and public life.

'In my end is my beginning'
MARY QUEEN OF SCOTS

'...the woman behaves like the Whore of Babylon'
JOHN KNOX

On the Trail of William Wallace

David R. Ross

ISBN 0 946487 47 2 PBK £7.99

How close to reality was *Braveheart*?

Where was Wallace actually born?

What was the relationship between Wallace and Bruce?

Are there any surviving eyewitness accounts of Wallace?

How does Wallace influence the psyche of today's Scots?

On the Trail of William Wallace offers a refreshing insight into the life and heritage of the great Scots hero whose proud story is at the very heart of what it means to be Scottish. Not concentrating simply on the hard historical facts of Wallace's life, the book also takes into account the real significance of Wallace and his effect on the ordinary Scot through the ages, manifested in the many sites where his memory is marked.

In trying to piece together the jigsaw of the reality of Wallace's life, David Ross weaves a subtle flow of new information with his own observations. His engaging, thoughtful and at times amusing narrative reads with the ease of a historical novel, complete with all the intrigue, treachery and romance required to hold the attention of the casual reader and still entice the more knowledgable historian.

74 places to visit in Scotland and the north of England

One general map and 3 location maps

Stirling and Falkirk battle plans

Wallace's route through London

Chapter on Wallace connections in North America and elsewhere

Reproductions of rarely seen illustrations

David Ross is organiser of and historical adviser to the Society of William Wallace.

'Historians seem to think all there is to be known about Wallace has already been uncovered. Mr Ross has proved that Wallace studies are in fact in their infancy.' ELSPETH KING, Director the Stirling Smith Art Museum & Gallery, who annotated and introduced the recent Luath edition of *Blind Harry's Wallace*.

On the Trail of John Wesley

J. Keith Cheetham

ISBN 1 84282 023 0 PBK £7.99

John Wesley (1703-91) founded the Methodist movement, initially an offshoot of the Church of England, which grew into a major church in its own right. In doing so Wesley brought about the greatest religious revival of the 18th century.

The name Methodism derives from the methodical approach Wesley adopted from the bible for developing personal devotion. His decision to employ lay preachers and preach outdoor sermons on the Word of God to a mainly working-class population angered the Church of England. It led to a split and in 1795, after John Wesley's death, the Methodist Church was established.

Wesley travelled over 250,000 miles across Britain, mainly on horseback, preaching over 40,000 sermons during his lifetime, often facing fierce opposition and persecution. He also spent two years in Georgia, USA, and was author and publisher of much religious material. His work and preaching was known to every branch of society.

Today the Methodist Church has spread to almost every country in the world with a membership of some 70 million.

Keith Cheetham traces Wesley's life story and gives detailed information on important Methodist heritage sites and places visited by the great preacher and evangelist.

Over 170 places to visit in Britain and Georgia, USA

One general map, and 7 location maps of Wesley's London, England, Scotland, Wales, Ireland and Georgia

Line drawings plus cross-references to maps throughout text

On the Trail of John Wesley is a thorough guide to the life and places connected with a man whose work and achievements changed the religious face of Britain and established the worldwide Methodist Church.

As well as being a biography, the book is a guide to over 200 Methodist-related sites in both Britain and America.

EXPRESS & STAR

... an enjoyably readable account of John Wesley's journeyings... a comprehensive and thoroughly useful handbook....

METHODIST RECORDER

On the Trail of Bonnie Prince Charlie

David R. Ross

ISBN 0 946487 68 5 PBK £7.99

On the Trail of Bonnie Prince Charlie is the story of the Young Pretender. Born in Italy, grandson of James VII, at a time when the German house of Hanover was on the throne, his father was regarded by many as the righful king. Bonnie Prince Charlie's campaign to retake the throne in his father's name changed the fate of Scotland. The Jacobite movement was responsible for the '45 Uprising, one of the most decisive times in Scottish history. The suffering following the battle of Culloden in 1746 still evokes emotion. Charles' own journey immediately after Culloden is well known: hiding in the heather, escaping to Skye with Flora MacDonald. Little known of is his return to London in 1750 incognito, where he converted to Protestantism (he re-converted to Catholicism before he died and is buried in the Vatican). He was often unwelcome in Europe after the failure of the uprising and came to hate any mention of Scotland and his lost chance.

79 places to visit in Scotland and England

One general map and 4 location maps

Prestonpans, Clifton, Falkirk and Culloden battle plans

Simplified family tree

Rarely seen illustrations

Yet again popular historian David R. Ross brings his own style to one of Scotland's most famous figures. Bonnie Prince Charlie is part of the folklore of Scotland. He brings forth feelings of antagonism from some and romanticism from others, but all agree on his legal right to the throne.

Knowing the story behind the place can bring the landscape to life. Take this book with you on your travels and follow the route taken by Charles' forces on their doomed march.

'Ross writes with an immediacy, a dynamism, that makes his subjects come alive on the page.'

DUNDEE COURIER

On the Trail of Robert the Bruce

David R. Ross

ISBN 0 946487 52 9 PBK £7.99

On the Trail of Robert the Bruce charts the story of Scotland's hero-king from his boyhood, through his days of indecision as Scotland suffered under the English yoke, to his assumption of the crown exactly six months after the death of William Wallace. Here is the astonishing blow by blow account of how, against fearful odds, Bruce led the Scots to win their greatest ever victory. Bannockburn was not the end of the story. The war against English oppression lasted another fourteen years. Bruce lived just long enough to see his dreams of an independent Scotland come to fruition in 1328 with the signing of the Treaty of Edinburgh. The trail takes us to Bruce sites in Scotland, many of the little known and forgotten battle sites in northern England, and as far afield as the Bruce monuments in Andalusia and Jerusalem.

67 places to visit in Scotland and elsewhere.

One general map, 3 location maps and a map of Bruce-connected sites in Ireland.

Bannockburn battle plan.

Drawings and reproductions of rarely seen illustrations.

On the Trail of Robert the Bruce is not all blood and gore. It brings out the love and laughter, pain and passion of one of the great eras of Scottish history. Read it and you will understand why David Ross has never knowingly killed a spider in his life. Once again, he proves himself a master of the popular brand of hands-on history that made *On the Trail of William Wallace* so popular.

'David R. Ross is a proud patriot and unashamed romantic.'

SCOTLAND ON SUNDAY

'Robert the Bruce knew Scotland, knew every class of her people, as no man who ruled her before or since has done. It was he who asked of her a miracle - and she accomplished it.'

AGNES MUIR MACKENZIE

On the Trail of Robert Burns

John Cairney

ISBN 0 946487 51 0 PBK £7.99

Is there anything new to say about Robert Burns?

John Cairney says it's time to trash Burns the Brand and come on the trail of the real Robert Burns. He is the best of travelling companions on this convivial, entertaining journey to the heart of the Burns story.

Internationally known as 'the face of Robert Burns', John Cairney believes that the traditional Burns tourist trail urgently needs to find a new direction. In an acting career spanning forty years he has often lived and breathed Robert Burns on stage. *On the Trail of Robert Burns* shows just how well he can get under the skin of a character. This fascinating journey around Scotland is a rediscovery of Scotland's national bard as a flesh and blood genius.

On the Trail of Robert Burns outlines five tours, mainly in Scotland. Key sites include:

Alloway – Burns' birthplace. 'Tam O' Shanter' draws on the witch-stories about Alloway Kirk first heard by Burns in his childhood.

Mossgiel – between 1784 and 1786 in a phenomenal burst of creativity Burns wrote some of his most memorable poems including 'Holy Willie's Prayer' and 'To a Mouse.'

Kilmarnock – the famous Kilmarnock edition of *Poems Chiefly in the Scottish Dialect* published in 1786.

Edinburgh – fame and Clarinda (among others) embraced him.

Dumfries – Burns died at the age of 37. The trail ends at the Burns mausoleum in St Michael's churchyard.

'For me an aim I never fash
I rhyme for fun'.
ROBERT BURNS

'My love affair on stage with Burns started in London in 1959. It was consumated on stage at the Traverse Theatre in Edinburgh in 1965 and has continued happily ever since'.

JOHN CAIRNEY

'The trail is expertly, touchingly and amusingly followed'. THE HERALD

On the Trail of Scotland's Myths and Legends

Stuart McHardy

ISBN: 1 84282 049 4 PBK 7.99

Who were the people who built the megaliths?

What great warriors sleep beneath the Hollow Hills?

Were the early Scottish saints just pagans in disguise?

Was King Arthur really Scottish?

When was Nessie first sighted?

This is a book about Scotland drawn from hundreds, if not thousands of years of storytelling. From the oral traditions of the Scots, Gaelic and Norse speakers of the past, it presents a new picture of who the Scottish are and where they come from. The stories that McHardy recounts may be hilarious, tragic, heroic, frightening or just plain bizzare, but they all provide an insight into a unique tradition of myth, legend and folklore that has marked both the language and landscape of Scotland.

On the Trail of Queen Victoria in the Highlands

Ian R. Mitchell

ISBN 0 946487 79 0 UK £7.99

How many Munros did Queen Victoria bag?

What 'essential services' did John Brown perform for Victoria?

(and why was Albert always tired?)

How many horses (to the nearest hundred) were needed to undertake a Royal Tour?

What happens when you send a Marxist on the tracks of Queen Victoria in the Highlands? – you get a book somewhat more interesting than the usual run of the mill royalist biographies!

Ian R. Mitchell took up the challenge of attempting to write with critical empathy on the peregrinations of Vikki Regina in the Highlands, and about her residence at Balmoral, through which a neo-feudal fairyland was created on Upper Deeside. The expeditions, social rituals and iconography of that world are explored and exploded from within, in what Mitchell terms a Bolshevisation of Balmorality. He follows in Victoria's footsteps throughout the Cairngorms and beyond, to the further reaches of the Highlands. On this journey, a grudging respect and even affection for Vikki ('the best of the bunch') emerges.

The book is designed to enable the armchair/ motorised reader, or walker, to follow in the steps of the most widely-travelled royal personage in the Highlands since Bonnie Prince Charlie had wandered there a century earlier.

Index map and 12 detailed maps

21 walks in Victoria's footsteps

Rarely seen Washington Wilson photographs

Colour and black and white reproductions of contemporary paintings

On the Trail of Queen Victoria in the Highlands will also appeal to those with an interest in the social and cultural history of Scotland and the Highlands – and the author, ever-mindful of his own 'royalties', hopes the declining band of monarchists might also be persuaded to give the book a try. There has never been a book on Victoria like this. It is especially topical with the centenary of her death falling in 2001.

Mountain writer and historian. Joint winner of the Boardman-Tasker Prize for Mountain Literature in 1991, and winner of the Outdoor Writer's Guild's Outdoor Book of the Year award in 1999.

'entertaining and well researched... Mitchell, a distinguished historian with several books under his belt, writes with substantial first-hand experience of the rigors of walking in Scotland's more ot less trackless spaces' the times weekend

'...will give you much to think about next time you're up that mountain.' THE GUARDIAN, on Scotland's Mountains before the Mountaineers.

On the Trail of John Muir

Cherry Good
ISBN 0 946487 62 6
PBK £7.99

Follow the man who made the US go green. Confidant of presidents, father of American National Parks,

trailblazer of world conservation and voted a Man of the Millennium in the US, John Muir's life and work is of continuing relevance. A man ahead of his time who saw the wilderness he loved threatened by industrialisation and determined to protect it, a crusade in which he was largely successful. His love of the wilderness began at an early age and he was filled with wanderlust all his life.

'Only by going in silence, without baggage, can on truly get into the heart of the wilderness. All other travel is mere dust and hotels and baggage and chatter.'
JOHN MUIR

Braving mosquitoes and black bears Cherry Good set herself on his trail – Dunbar, Scotland; Fountain Lake and Hickory Hill, Wisconsin; Yosemite Valley and the Sierra Nevada, California; the Grand Canyon, Arizona; Alaska; and Canada – to tell his story. John Muir was himself a prolific writer, and Good draws on his books, articles, letters and diaries to produce an account that is lively, intimate, humorous and anecdotal, and that provides refreshing new insights into the hero of world conservation.

John Muir chronology

General map plus 10 detailed maps covering the US, Canada and Scotland

Original colour photographs

Afterword advises on how to get involved

Conservation websites and addresses

Muir's importance has long been acknowledged in the US with over 200 sites of scenic beauty named after him. He was a Founder of The Sierra Club which now has over ½ million members. Due to the movement he started some 360 million acres of wilderness are now protected. This is a book which shows Muir not simply as a hero but as likeable humorous and self-effacing man of extraordinary vision.

'I do hope that those who read this book will burn with the same enthusiasm for John Muir which the author shows.'
WEST HIGHLAND FREE PRESS

Luath Press Limited

committed to publishing well written books worth reading

LUATH PRESS takes its name from Robert Burns, whose little collie Luath (*Gael.*, swift or nimble) tripped up Jean Armour at a wedding and gave him the chance to speak to the woman who was to be his wife and the abiding love of his life. Burns called one of *The Twa Dogs* Luath after Cuchullin's hunting dog in *Ossian's Fingal*. Luath Press grew up in the heart of Burns country, and now resides a few steps up the road from Burns' first lodgings in Edinburgh's Royal Mile.

Luath offers you distinctive writing with a hint of unexpected pleasures.

Most UK and US bookshops either carry our books in stock or can order them for you. To order direct from us, please send a £sterling cheque, postal order, international money order or your credit card details (number, address of cardholder and expiry date) to us at the address below. Please add post and packing as follows: UK – £1.00 per delivery address; overseas surface mail – £2.50 per delivery address; overseas airmail – £3.50 for the first book to each delivery address, plus £1.00 for each additional book by airmail to the same address. If your order is a gift, we will happily enclose your card or message at no extra charge.

Luath Press Limited
543/2 Castlehill
The Royal Mile
Edinburgh EH1 2ND
Scotland
Telephone: 0131 225 4326 (24 hours)
Fax: 0131 225 4324
email: gavin.macdougall@luath.co.uk
Website: www.luath.co.uk